SONG IN THE
NIGHT

By: James Moody

Trilogy Christian Publishers
A Wholly Owned Subsidiary of Trinity Broadcasting Network
2442 Michelle Drive
Tustin, CA 92780
Copyright © 2022 by James Franklin Moody
Used by permission. All rights reserved worldwide.
Scripture quotations marked (KJV) taken from The Holy Bible,
King James Version. Cambridge Edition: 1769.
All rights reserved, including the right to reproduce this book or
portions thereof in any form whatsoever.
For information, address Trilogy Christian Publishing
Rights Department, 2442 Michelle Drive, Tustin, Ca 92780.
Trilogy Christian Publishing/ TBN and colophon are trademarks
of Trinity Broadcasting Network.
For information about special discounts for bulk purchases,
please contact Trilogy Christian Publishing.
Manufactured in the United States of America

10 9 8 7 6 5 4 3 2 1
Library of Congress Cataloging-in-Publication Data is available.
ISBN 978-1-63769-654-5
ISBN 978-1-63769-655-2 (ebook)

DEDICATION

To my mother and father, without whose love I would not have
life, nor would I have learned of *eternal* life.

"I call to remembrance my song in the night..." (Psalm 77:6, KJV).

TABLE OF CONTENTS

PREFACE

—◆—

This is a story I've been trying to write for twenty-five years. But it just wasn't time...until now. Why was I never able to do it (even though I tried many times)? Who can tell? Who can fathom the ways of an almighty God? I can't. All we can do is obey when He speaks. That's why I know that this is the right time for this story. It all simply came together one cold Virginia February afternoon. In fact, I know that now is the time because He wrote it, really. He started writing it when I was a child.

If I had to choose for myself, I would have written a far different story. No one would choose some of the experiences found in this book (though they are by no means the worst that some humans have endured). Humans naturally seek out the comfortable, the pleasant, and the enjoyable experiences in life. For all of our technology, education, and "freedom," we don't really have as much choice about how our life plays out as we may think.

But in a sense, I *did* choose this life when I said a prayer to God. It was a simple prayer. There was nothing profound or complicated about it. It wasn't a prayer written in flowery language or Shakespearean English. But it was a prayer I made with every fiber of who

I was at the time.

The prayer was simply, "Not *my* will be done, Lord, but *Your* will be done in my life."

And it was then that things in my life began to change...*dramatically*. What followed that prayer is just as amazing to me as anything I have read in fiction. It was just as unplanned by me and as remarkable as if I had been living in a true Hollywood adventure movie. It wasn't always easy, of course, and not as straightforward as a ninety-minute film, but it was no less remarkable. But *that* story is for another time. *This* story you hold in your hands is all about how I got to the point of making that prayer.

And this is why I say that this story before you is not something *I* have written. I've simply followed the Leader. Now, I simply serve as a secretary, recording and describing for you what the God of heaven has been doing with a life that is surrendered fully to Him. My choice was to give Him that control. *His* choice was to take me on this remarkable adventure stretching from some of the darkest places in the human heart to some of the most glorious heights. I could never have planned it, nor would I *like* to have planned it. I prefer letting God do that.

Life is a mystery. It can't always be planned out decades in advance (though I tried). Things don't always work out the way we hope (though we tell ourselves they will). But mystery is good. Mystery makes life all the more interesting and worthwhile.

Who would want to know everything they may encounter in life—both the good and the bad? There would be no pleasant surprises to enjoy, such as an unexpected and welcome relationship. And who would want to know that a period of struggle or illness lay ahead? One might be tempted to give up before it comes and never get to experience the triumph of victory. The mysterious aspects of life can add excitement to an otherwise rather boring, mundane existence. And God is definitely *not* boring!

And when our lives are wholly surrendered to the One who numbers every hair on our heads, He takes us in hand along a journey of adventure. There will be challenges, yes, but there are also joys beyond measure.

Well, this story is about how that truth came to be engraved upon my heart when God wrote these truths into my life.

Whatever the challenges we face, those who have surrendered their lives fully to Jesus Christ can be assured that no matter what happens—in all the ups and downs of the Christian pilgrimage—God does not forsake us. And God will always make sure that whatever comes along that is meant to convince you to give up is turned around for your good and for your healing if your will is surrendered to the will of God.

Because that is God's main business—healing. That is the purpose of the cross of Jesus and of the resurrection. It is the reason for the empty tomb—to bring healing to the lost, hopeless, and wounded. He's a healer, and He's very good at it. He's done it before. He's done it for me. And He will do it for you.

James Moody

Note: While some names have been changed, dialogue supplemented, and time elements re-arranged, the events of this story are true (JM).

CHAPTER 1

Christmas on Elm Street

The Christmas holiday had arrived. It was the first full day out of school, and the skies had dumped enough snow on the ground for the neighborhood boys to declare a snowball war. Energies ran high, as would be expected, when that long-awaited day of freedom came. At least for two weeks, the constraints of class and clock were gone, and in their place came the heated expectation of the Yuletide season, presents under the tree, and family gatherings. The boys could now escape into the great outdoors.

For the boys, the "great outdoors" happened to be a sprawling cemetery just blocks away from the capitol building in Raleigh, North Carolina. Except, *this* graveyard was one of those grand Victorian inventions by city planners—it served the dual purpose of burying the dead and providing room to amble for the living.

Oakwood Cemetery was by no means full of gravesites alone. In addition to its quiet monuments dedicated to southern American history-makers, there were large open fields that were just right for kite-flying, bike-riding, and army battles. No boy could ask for a more exciting terrain to explore than that provided by the creekbeds, ancient oaks, and large storm-drain tunnels.

"He's over there, behind the tree!" someone shouted. Snow-balls bombarded the area, mostly hitting the tree.

"Yes!" He made a fist and jerked his arm down in a triumphant gesture. "We're winning!"

"No, you're not. You guys were hit more than *us*!"

"No, we weren't!" shouted one of the boys. A minor disagreement erupted, signaling the need for truce talks.

The sun's light waned, thanks to the lingering clouds and the general time of year. Steve glanced at his watch.

"Hey, we've got to go. It's almost five o'clock."

The boys gave up the last of their ammunition, but not until letting a few extra shots fly post-truce. They each picked up their bikes from the side of the hill, pushed them onto the roads, and mounted them, riding off one by one or in pairs. Though the roads were treacherous to ride on at the time, they could not resist biking in the snow.

James was the last to reach his bike. He picked it up and started following behind the others, some of whom had already sped ahead. The more daring of them slammed on their brakes when reaching thick patches of snow on the road, just to see how far they could slide. James carried on walking his bike towards the gate.

About fifty feet away from the large stone and wrought-iron entrance, he stopped. He looked over to a small black gravestone lying at an angle on the ground. It was not one of the large, expensive shrines like the others. It was simple, plain, and small. It sat under a large tree, so not much snow had collected on top of it. He walked over to it, though, reached down, and brushed away what snow was there. His eyes fixed on its inscription, and the cold air of December seemed to take hold of his throat. A slight breeze tousled the bangs of his hair that were hanging out from underneath his woolly toboggan. He calculated the age of the boy whose bones lay beneath. *Eleven...no...twelve years old*, he thought to himself.

"That's the same age as me," he said out loud. As the chill of the late afternoon entered his airway, he became conscious of the cold air pouring into his lungs. He couldn't move. His eyes would not blink. It is as if he were staring beyond the gravestone into another world, and he stood immovable while feelings he could not explain hit him like the cold waves on the shore of the Outer Banks off the Carolina coast.

"I wonder what it's like to..."

A fresh snowball hit him on the back and brought him back to the world of a bleak and frigid day, back to the outside of himself, back to the harsh reality of winter.

"Come on, James!" Steve said, more annoyed than impatient. "Mom said that Granny and Grandpa were coming over today. They're probably there by now!"

Pushing their bikes up the steep hill to their house one block away, they passed by their church sitting on the corner of Polk and Elm Streets, a red brick building taking up a fourth of that city block. The soft white of the street lights lit up the historic neighborhood, just as it may have appeared in the Victorian age under

13

gas lamps when most of those houses were first built. Reaching the back of the house by way of the alley next to it, they saw the car of their grandparents sitting in the driveway. They rushed to put their bikes on the back porch and ran through the backdoor.

"Hey Granny! Hi Grandpa!"

"Well, hey there, boys," Grandpa answered. "Looks like you've been rolling around in the snow out there! What have you been up to?" He was technically a step-grandfather, whom they usually called by his first name, Reece, but as far as the boys were concerned, he was the grandfather, the one closest to them. The retired North Carolina civil servant always showed enthusiasm and interest in whatever the boys were doing.

"We had a snowball fight with Doug and Jake and some of the other guys. It was great. You should've seen the snowdrifts down by the creek!" Steve explained.

"Were they big?" he asked.

"Gigantic," James explained, using his hands and arms as visual aids to show their size.

"You boys shouldn't be out in this cold weather," Granny interrupted in her reproving voice. Her reprimand was in a pleading manner as if their offense would cause her untold heartaches. "You could pick up a cold right here at Christmas."

She opened her arms, expecting a hug, and James walked over to fill them. To her, he was "Jimmy," so-named after her own father. She squeezed him tightly and kissed him on the cheek. "Are you glad to be out of school now?"

"Oh yes!" he said without hesitation. "Are you and Reece here to stay through to New Year's Day?"

"We wouldn't be anywhere else now, would we?" She drew him close again and gave him another hug and kiss. After looking at him for a second, her eyes narrowed briefly, and she looked more carefully through her black-rimmed glasses.

"What's that on your neck?" she asked the boy, gently lifting his chin with her hand.

"What's what?" he said.

"On your neck...that little bump?"

"I don't know. Never noticed it."

After dismissing it by way of a smile, she leaned down to his ear and whispered, "I left something for you under your pillow." She straightened back up, nodded slightly, and winked.

At that moment, the aluminum storm door at the back of the house swung open again, and everyone could shortly hear the closing of it along with the inside door, a big, old wooden leftover from Victorian times. The deadbolt lock slid shut, and the sound of a coat being taken off came from the back hall.

Steve was explaining to Reece all the details of the battle down at the cemetery. Barbara, the boys' mother, was busy cooking while telling her mother of all the mundane, ordinary events of the past week in the Moody household.

Charles, the husband and father, walked into the kitchen and greeted his in-laws in a friendly manner that underlay the warm and genuine relationship he had with them.

"Rose, Reece, how you folks doing?"

"Oh fine, just fine, Charles. Can't complain," Reece said. "How about you?"

"'Bout the same."

He walked over to James, now sitting at the kitchen table, and stuck his cold hand down the nape of his neck.

"Dad!"

"What?" Charles said innocently.

"Don't! That's so cold!"

The father smiled, walked over to the counter while greeting his wife, and began to pour himself a cup of coffee.

"Do you want a cup, Reece?" he asked.

"Thank you, Charles; you know, I think I will have just a little." Then, in a dry and deadpan tone, he added, "Charles, you know I've started working on my second million now?" Charles didn't bat an eye or look up while pouring. He simply carried on.

"Oh yeah?"

"Yep." Reece paused for effect. "I gave up on my *first* million." He chuckled.

"Oh, Reece! Don't be like that," Granny reproved again.

The two men struck up a conversation about the events of the day, the latest political news, and the state of the economy. They soon retired to the "den" to watch television, enjoy their coffee, and carry on their talks.

As they left the kitchen, Granny walked over to her daughter and spoke in a low tone.

"Do you know what that is on James' neck?" she asked.

"No, I haven't seen anything. What are you talking about, Mother?"

"There's a little lump there, Bobbie. I think you should have it looked at."

"I'll look at it later. I'm sure it's nothing. Probably just an insect bite or something like that."

She carried on preparing the dinner, and Granny helped to set the table. Steve followed the men into the den. James ran to his bedroom, looked under the pillow of his bed, and found a five-dollar bill.

CHAPTER 2

New Impressions

Several weeks later, school was back in full swing. Basketball season had started, and James was anything but a sportsman. But his brother was. So, Friday nights were taken up with hanging around the school gym, watching the game, and looking to see who else showed up back at school at the end of a long school week.

"Go on, James. I bet you she'll talk to you," John said.

"No. There's no chance of that happening. I already made *that* mistake."

Though the same age, John had already begun the quick sprint of adolescence, while James hadn't yet started. His friend was about one foot taller already. He had a voice to match.

They were both looking at the one girl James had never lost sight of since he arrived at the school in fourth grade. She was pretty and kind but always seemed just out of his reach for anything more than being casual friends. She was as charming a southern girl as any southern boy could dream of being with, but she was so pleasant to everyone, and no one guy ever seemed to enjoy more of her attention than another. Once, when they were all at the skating rink one Saturday, he remembered pretending to have to hold on to the rail and skate slowly, just so he could follow behind her, hoping they might bump into one another or that he'd be able to help her up after a fall.

"She's nice to me, John. But she's nice to everybody. She always is. I'm just a classmate, like you!"

"Well, maybe so. But I know one thing—I'm sure not going to wait around forever to talk to someone *I* like."

The crowd in the stands began to cheer. Steve had made another goal—a perfect three-pointer, pushing the Bulldog team over the top to win the game in the last couple of minutes. His mom, in the stands a few bleachers up, shouted out, "That's my boy!"

James looked at John, raised his eyebrows, and then looked down to the ground.

• • •

Saturday morning cartoons, Saturday afternoon games in the backyard with friends, Sunday morning church, and Sunday afternoon dinner at home all flew by quickly. Monday morning came, and it was time to get up and start the week once again. James turned off the alarm, sat up in bed, and swung his feet over the side as he sat there a few seconds, trying to wake up fully.

While mustering the energy to stand up, thinking about nothing in particular, he suddenly became aware of a word being impressed on his mind. It wasn't a voice, necessarily, but more like an idea that just popped into his consciousness: "I have called you to be a seer to my people."

It took him by surprise but didn't startle him. It just lingered there, like what a person might see when closing his eyes after looking at a bright light—except it wasn't something he saw but something he intuitively knew. The afterglow of a peaceful presence, along with this idea, just simmered inside of him.

"A seer?" he said to himself. "That's weird. I wonder what that is."

After showering and dressing, he sat down to breakfast with his brother and mom.

"Mom, what's a seer?"

"A what?"

"A seer."

Steve offered an answer, "That's easy. It's someone who works at *SE-ers*, duh!"

"I don't think so," James answered, a little annoyed.

"I don't know, James. Sounds like something from the Bible to me. I have a Bible dictionary behind my desk you can look it up in. But you don't have time right now. Finish up. We need to leave early and pick up Linda on the way to school. Her mom's car is broken down."

The eight-mile ride in their mother's used Pacer took the usual ten or fifteen minutes through Raleigh's morning traffic. After the other two got out of the car in front of the school, his mother stopped James for a minute.

"Oh, I forgot to tell you, James. I'll be picking you up at lunch-time. We have an appointment to see a doctor."

"But what about my paper route after school?" he asked.

"Don't worry. It won't take long. We'll be finished before *that*. It's just a check-up."

He shut the door and slung his backpack over his shoulder and headed to class. Barbara drove off back home. When she arrived, she parked the car on the street in front of the house and walked up the seven or eight steps to the front door.

Their house, built in the late 1800s, was bought by her and Charles when the neighborhood was not part of a historic renovation trend but rather part of the downtown area all the well-to-do folks had moved away from. Then, a few preservationists moved back in to start saving these gems of the town. Their house, 415 Elm Street, had been in various stages of renovation through the years. Unlike many of the other owners who completed renovations within a year, Charles and Barbara worked on different parts when they could afford to, which took many years altogether. By the time the two youngest boys were in junior high school, the basic work had been completed. The outside was finished, and most of the inside walls and floors had been re-furbished. Even the interior had been decorated by Barbara herself. She excelled in design and had been told more than once by friends and family that she had missed one of her callings in life—an interior decorator.

As she put the key in the front door lock on that sunny morning, she was stopped in her tracks by an impression that flooded into her mind and spirit, a voice that seemed to rise up from within: "Do not look on the outward appearance of what I am going to do. This is a work of eternal value." Tears came to her eyes as she recognized this gentle voice. She didn't entirely comprehend the ramifications of this intuitive knowledge, and she was not sure of what was being communicated to her, but she rushed inside to hide away in her place of prayer.

• • •

At one o'clock, Barbara and James were sitting in Dr. Sparrow's office, an ear, nose, and throat specialist. He examined James' neck where the small lump appeared. He looked down the boy's throat, asked a few questions, and prodded and poked as most doctors do.

"Has he been stung by a bee lately?"

"I don't think so, Dr. Sparrow. I can't remember that happening. Can you, James?"

"No."

"Has he had any other symptoms like bumps, swellings, or itching? You're not allergic to anything, are you, James?"

"Not that I know of."

"I haven't seen anything, Doctor. And this thing has been around since before Christmas. That's when my mother first noticed it. Nothing has changed since then," Barbara explained.

Doctor Sparrow, a gentle man with very soft hands and a voice of the same quality, put both hands on the boy's neck to feel for other bumps or nodules. After a few seconds, he looked at the boy, smiled, and patted him on the shoulder. He picked the file of paperwork back up and walked over to the door.

"Mrs. Moody, may I talk to you outside for just a minute?"

• • •

Later that evening, the family sat in the kitchen eating dinner.

"Surgery?" Charles questioned. "Does he think that's really necessary?"

"That's what he said," Barbara replied. (Most of her family members referred to her as Bobbie.) "It's the only way to find out what this thing is. But it's only an exploratory surgery. He'll just open it up and have a look around. They'll take out a specimen to be sent away for analysis. He said it's not a complicated procedure."

The boy's dad didn't say anything further but picked around at his food.

A few minutes later, he chimed back into the conversation that was rambling in several directions. "When does he want to do this, Bobbie?"

"As soon as possible, maybe even next week."

Everyone finished eating while talking about other things—the upcoming basketball game, homework assignments, or what was happening at the church youth group that week.

After each one finished, they took their plates to the sink and left Mom to do the cleaning up.

"James, don't forget. Your piano lesson is tomorrow. You need to practice right now."

"But Mom! I don't *want* to do it now; I have..."

"Half an hour! Get to it. No excuses."

He gave out a very loud sigh and walked into the living room just next to the kitchen.

The old, cherry-stained upright piano, with its tinny saloon sound and yellowed ivory keys, sat in the corner. He sat down on the circular stool and opened his book to the latest piece his teacher had given him to learn, "Gatlinburg Boogie." He looked at his watch to mark the time he started, making sure not to practice too long.

The piece was disjointed and erratic: a sour note here, a good riff there, but nothing that flowed together yet. Halfway through a line, his impatience took over, and he hit as many keys as he could in exasperation. His father stuck his head around the corner.

"Syncopation. Remember: *sync-o-pa-tion*!"

His father wasn't musical at all. And James didn't even know what the word meant. He ignored the instructions and tried to concentrate on just hitting the right notes.

CHAPTER 3

———

The Day Arrives

"Yes, Dr. Sparrow has scheduled the operation for next Thursday....No, he won't be in more than two nights....Hold on a minute, Pansy, I need to turn this chicken over."

Barbara placed the phone on the kitchen table. It was early afternoon. The boys were still in school, and the sun was shining brightly in the side window of the kitchen. She reached over to the frying pan, adjusted the meat, picked the phone back up, and resumed her conversation.

"It won't leave him too weak. There really isn't much the doctor will do except to take out a little bit of whatever he finds for a biopsy."

The voice on the other end of the phone line was her sister.

"What does that involve?"

"Well, he'll just make a small incision in his neck and take out what he needs. James will have a small scar, but that's about all."

"We'll certainly be praying for you all."

"Yes, we do need your prayers."

"Bobbie, I know this sounds strange, but I felt this morning that James should start to sing."

"What? What do you mean, 'sing'?"

"I mean 'to sing.' Perhaps that is something God wants him to do. He started to take piano lessons, didn't he? Well, maybe he should try singing also. If he can play, then maybe he can sing too."

"That's the only thing that you sensed when praying this morning?"

"Well, yes. But I think it's important."

"Maybe so, but it sounds like an odd thing when the boy is having his throat operated on of all places, doesn't it?"

"You will tell him, won't you?"

"Yes, I'll tell him, maybe after this ordeal is over." She paused to catch a breath. "So, is Floyd in the state this week, or is he out of town?"

"No, he's driving his truck up to New York this week. I've ridden with him in that eighteen-wheeler around New York. There's so much traffic there; I don't like him having to drive that far away."

"I'm sure you don't. I know he gets tired of being on the road all the time."

● ● ●

Homeroom had just ended. Students were milling around their lockers, talking, making plans for the weekend, and some were even getting books ready for the next class. James and John walked out of their classroom.

"Yeah, Mom says I'll only be out of school a couple of days."

"That sounds like fun!" John looked excited by the prospect. "Then all you'll have to do is lay around in bed watching TV. I could do with some of that right now."

"Oh yeah!" James replied sarcastically. "Lots of fun. I can't wait!"

The boys stopped at their lockers to get their books for the next class. John fumbled with the combination lock until he finally managed to open it up on the third try.

"Hey, James, you play the piano, don't you?"

"Not really well. I only started taking lessons a couple of years ago. Why?"

"Well, you know the Fine Arts Festival is coming up. You should think about entering it."

"I don't know about that."

"I'm going to try for a solo with my trombone."

"A solo? The trombone really isn't something you play a solo with, is it?"

"Sure. You'll see. There's a great jazz piece I'm learning."

"Well, better you than me. Besides, my arms aren't as long as yours. I'd never be able to stretch far enough for those low notes!"

The late bell rang. Everyone in the hallways scattered, running in the direction of their next classes before the doors were shut.

Students in the hallways opened the doors that were shut as slowly and as quietly as they could, trying not to be heard.

• • •

Next week came too soon. In youth, time seems to move so slowly, and students always watch the clock in that last period of school until three o'clock arrives and the bell rings. Christmas seems so far away when you begin the school year; summer seems even further. But when there is something you dread, something you're apprehensive about facing, the time seems to march quickly without delay. It was a week like that for James.

James and Barbara arrived at the hospital on a Thursday afternoon. The surgery would be the following morning. Until then, there was much to be accomplished: volumes of paperwork, numerous measurements, vials of blood-taking, and settling into a sterile room all had to be maneuvered through. There would be no dinner that night in preparation for operating early in the morning.

After the settling in time, Granny (who bore the name "Rose," presumably because it matched her pink cheeks) showed up along with Reece. James' dad, Charles, dropped in after getting off work at the barbershop (conveniently just a couple of miles away). Everyone was as upbeat and encouraging as possible. The talk was light, and Reece's ever-active sense of humor kept everyone in stitches (much to Rose's dismay). But they eventually had to leave for the night.

It was only the second time James had been in the hospital. The first time was for a minor operation. But this night felt different.

He was younger the first time, and it didn't leave much of an impression on him. This time, though, fear began to wriggle its way into the boy's mind. The sounds and smells of the hospital did their best to help keep him awake and anxious about the coming operation. Sleep was sporadic, infrequent, and fretful.

Early in the morning, a nurse came in for the pre-operation shot. The family arrived soon after. And the effects of the shot came just after that. He began to feel more relaxed but also acquired a mouth as dry as a southern cotton ball.

His mom and grandmother were there as the team came to place him on the gurney and roll him down to the operating room. His mother walked with him as far as she was allowed to go. They wheeled him into the operating room, lifted him off the gurney, and placed him on the table.

"All right, James. This won't take long," Dr. Sparrow comforted. Of course, it was hard to tell it was Dr. Sparrow with that surgical mask on. It was only his kind, gentle voice that gave him away. "Are you ready for us to start this?"

"Yes," the boy answered drowsily.

"Okay, nurse," the doctor said to the assistant.

A female voice spoke comfortingly: "James, you'll feel a tiny prick in your arm while we put the IV in, okay?"

After the momentary pain, a cold fluid began to travel around his body. Another doctor placed a breathing mask over his face and gave him instructions: "James, I want you to count backward from ten. Can you do that for me?"

"Ten...nine...eight...seven...six..."

• • •

A few hours later, still unconscious and with bandages on his neck, he was lying in his hospital room. His mom and grandmother were there. Dr. Sparrow walked into the room, still wearing his green surgical garb. He was somber and hesitant but resolved to carry out his duty.

The two women both stood up to greet him. But they knew by the lack of eye contact what the message was.

"Mrs. Moody," he said in his quiet voice, "I believe it is always important to let my patients know from the start what to expect." He paused and waited until his words registered with the mother and daughter. "What I would say right now is, don't make any plans for the boy's immediate future."

Barbara's face froze. Her mother grabbed hold of her arm as she sat back down slowly on the chair.

"What do you mean, Doctor?"

"What I mean is that I am not encouraged by what we found. Of course, we are going to have to run the necessary tests and make absolutely sure of what is there, but I can tell you that this is going to be a hard battle."

"A battle? I thought you said it was probably just an allergic reaction...?"

"As you know, Mrs. Moody, that was just a preliminary analysis. That was just what I could tell by looking at his outward symptoms. But having opened up this part of his neck, I can tell you that I found something quite invasive. Of course, only the analysis will be more conclusive, but there is a mass in his neck."

"A mass? What do you mean, *mass*?"

Barbara's mother, who had worked as a nurse herself many years ago, asked, "Do you mean a tumor?"

"Yes, ma'am. But it isn't restricted to the front area of his neck where you saw the lump. What I could see while he was open, along with the scans we were able to take, show that it's growing to the back of the neck and up towards his brain. It's extensive. In fact, if I had tried to remove all of what I found, I would have disfigured his face for the rest of his life."

"Doctor, is this mass...is it malignant?" Rose asked.

"That's what the analysis will tell us. We've already sent the sample to the Armed Services Research Center, and they're best equipped to find out what it is."

"Yes, but is it *cancer*?"

"I can't tell you that, Mrs. Moody. All I can tell you is that we'll have to wait to hear the report. It won't be long before we know."

"Then what?" Rose asked.

"Well, after that I will confer with some of my colleagues and figure out what needs to be done next as a follow-up treatment." He paused for a few seconds. "Based on what I saw, however, all I can tell you is just be prepared."

Barbara looked at him, tears already beginning to trickle down her cheeks. "Prepared for what, Doctor?"

"What I'm telling you, Mrs. Moody is that we are going to do all we can for James. And we can use all the help we can get right now." He walked over to the boy, who was still deeply asleep. He glanced at the chart and put it back at the foot of the bed. He then walked over to the two women and took each of them by their hands. "Mrs. Moody, I know you're a praying woman, aren't you?"

"Yes, Dr. Sparrow."

"Then pray." His eyes penetrated hers as he paused. "Pray for a miracle."

He left the room. The two mothers embraced one another. James lay on the bed motionless, unconscious and unaware of all that was said.

CHAPTER 4

———◆———

A Gentle Hand

He was back at home Saturday. It didn't take long for him to recover from the simple procedure. His mother did not yet tell him anything of what the doctor had explained to her. She put that off until hearing a final report.

The bandage and scar were a novelty at school. Once the bandage came off, the stitches were soon to follow, but not before everyone had a good look at them.

"Did it hurt a lot?" John asked.

"Only the part when they took me into the operating room and stuck me in the arm."

"Man, that's a nice scar. You'll have that for the rest of your life, you know?"

"Yeah, I figured that out, John. The surgeon *did* say that he put it in the place where my wrinkles will hide it when I get older. A lot of good *that* does me now, huh?"

• • •

A few weeks later, his mom got the call.

"Mrs. Moody?"

"Yes."

"Hi, Mrs. Moody. This is Dr. Robertson. I'm an associate of Dr. Sparrow. We've been in contact, and he asked me to get in touch with you. Do you have a second?"

"Yes, Doctor, I do. Is this about the biopsy?"

"It is, yes. We have discussed James' results that came in yesterday. I was wondering if I could see you and him tomorrow morning."

"Tomorrow? But that's Saturday. Are you open on Saturday? I hate to make you come in on your day off if you have one."

"Don't worry about that, Mrs. Moody. I'll be in the office, and it will be quiet. We don't normally have patients in on the weekend, so no one else will be here. But I'll leave the outside door open for you. Now, do you know where Corporate Drive is out by the North Hills Shopping Mall?"

• • •

Saturday morning cartoons were off the menu that weekend. Barbara drove James and herself the five or six miles to the doctor's office near the mall.

It seemed like there was always a new shopping center or new business center popping up overnight in the city of Raleigh. The place had never ceased to grow since she and her husband moved there in the 1960s. Originally from the mill town of Roanoke Rapids, North Carolina, Barbara had moved to the town of New Bern at fourteen. It was there she met Charles when she was a junior in high school. He was born in Michigan, a mid-westerner, and a U.S. Marine at the Cherry Point Marine Corps Air Station near New Bern. They met at church one Sunday, began to date, and married shortly after her graduation. Afterward, they moved to Ohio for a short spell. But the charm of the South (and family) drew them back to the Old North State. They settled in the capital city where he began work as a barber, and she began life as a wife and landlord for the rental rooms in a house next door to them. She always said running that place was where she got *her* college education—an education in human nature. Now, sixteen years into the rearing of a family of three boys, the couple was facing a new challenge.

Barbara pulled into the parking lot of the professional offices that were mostly empty of cars. Dr. Robertson was right. It was *very* quiet that day. They made their way up the stairs from the side door and into an office marked by a sign: "Dr. Robertson, Oncologist."

As soon as the chime went off from opening the door to the outer office, a nurse appeared and showed them into an examination room. There was no one else in the waiting area and no receptionist. It was the first time either of them had an appointment with a doctor when they didn't have to wait at all. Nurse Sandy was the only other person around, and with a personality as bright as the sunshine, it was clear that the doctor knew how to hire the right kind of people to work with him in this profession.

Only seconds after they sat down, Dr. Robertson walked in and greeted them both with the same wonderful bedside manner of his colleague, Dr. Sparrow. Though a young man, he had a bushy beard that seemed to cover most of his face and more. James thought about the man on the wilderness nature program that came on TV Saturday mornings. All that was missing was the red-checked shirt and boots.

"Thank you for coming in on Saturday, Mrs. Moody. This is a quieter and easier day to meet like this. We don't have to put up with all the busyness of a regular day."

"Thank *you*, Dr. Robertson. I know this must be a sacrifice for you."

"Well, this is the kind of work that requires us all to do the best we can, especially in this type of medical practice. How are you feeling, James? Recovered from that operation on your neck?"

"Yes, I think so."

He smiled and put his hand on the boy's shoulder. He then sat down on the rolling stool just opposite the exam table where the boy sat. After a brief look at the boy's neck to see how the scar was healing, he moved his stool just a little bit away from the exam table. His expression changed as he looked down to the floor and paused for a few seconds. He put his hands together, fingertips touching one another, and raised his hands to his mouth briefly before removing them.

"Mrs. Moody, James, I'm sorry to tell you this, but the results that came back on Dr. Sparrow's biopsy were positive. What he found is a malignant cancer. The reason it took so long for us to get the results is because of the rarity of this disease. It's called a Nerve

Sheath Sarcoma. And it isn't easy to identify."

"A nerve what?"

"Nerve Sheath Sarcoma. That means it is a cancer that is in the nerve of that part of his head. It runs from the front and reaches to the back area of the brain."

"A nerve...the brain?" Barbara repeated slowly, not really understanding.

"In fact, it is quite rare. Only seven or eight cases have been recorded in medical history, which means, James, you've made history already in your life!" His weak smile betrayed the fact that he knew his good-effort attempt to lighten an already heavy situation would not help much to relieve the weight of what he was saying.

He stopped to get the box of tissues sitting on the table and handed several to Barbara. James sat on the table, hearing what the doctor was saying but not really taking it all in. In fact, the main thing he felt was numbness; he knew what the doctor was saying, but he wasn't really able to think beyond the moment.

"What do we do now, Doctor?"

"Well, I will be his primary oncologist, with you and your husband's agreement. I will confer with radiation specialists over at the hospital, and we'll put together a course of chemotherapy and radiotherapy to go after this thing aggressively. We will try to stop it. But, as I said, the course of treatment for this kind of cancer is uncertain. It just hasn't been encountered that often, so we don't know *for sure* what will be effective."

He looked at James, who sat with no expression on his face.

"James, do you understand what I'm saying?"

The boy nodded his head slightly but didn't say anything.

"So, you don't know if it will work. You can't tell us for sure?" Barbara asked.

"Nothing is for sure, Mrs. Moody. All I can tell you is that we will do our very best. But this will be a highly aggressive course of treatment, and it will be hard to get through it. It will be demanding and last for many months to come."

He turned to look at the boy alone. "James, this will require a lot out of you. I won't tell you it will be easy. But you've got to be prepared for a long fight, okay?"

The boy was not prepared to speak anymore. He simply acknowledged that the doctor was talking to him.

"We can only do our part, Mrs. Moody...and pray for help from above."

• • •

The family sat around the dinner table, finishing up what they could. Everyone was subdued, though. They tried to have some conversation about ordinary events of the day, but it was hard. The oldest of the three boys, Rick, was also there. He had recently married and moved out to his own home, a few miles away. He came over now and then.

"You know the Wolfpack might make it to the Final Four this

year?" Steve said.

"Could be," Rick answered. "I hear that Jimmy V has a trick or two up his sleeve."

"Maybe you'll be up there one day, Steve, playing basketball for the Wolfpack," Barbara offered.

"I don't know. I'm not really interested in going to college. I've been thinking about the Marines. What do you think, Dad? You were a Marine. What would you think if I went in too?"

"You could end up in a war, you know?" Rick said.

"Nah. He won't be in a war," Charles said. "I don't think there's one coming up too soon. You could do worse, Son."

"No freedom. Taking orders all the time. I don't know about that," Rick cautioned.

James, usually the slowest to finish eating, declined most of what was on his plate that night. He put his fork down and stood up. "I'm gonna go to my room. I'm not that hungry," he said.

No one said anything. His mother didn't force him to "clean his plate" as the usual instruction went if something was left uneaten. He put his plate on the counter and walked out. The conversation was more hushed.

"So it is cancer? Is he sure?" Charles asked.

"Yes, Charles. He's sure. But Dr. Robertson is one of the best oncologists in the area. They're putting together a course of treatment that they think will help."

"Help how much?" Rick asked.

"They don't know. It's a rare cancer, and the doctor said that the way to treat it is uncertain also."

James had gone to his room. Recently, it had become more of a retreat than just a place to sleep. One of his prized possessions was his new drafting table—a drawing table like the ones used by designers, architects, and artists. For years he had longed to have one of his own. It was the ideal workspace to draw, to create, to put together models, and to dream of creating new things. Having started a paper route at age nine in one of the office buildings of downtown Raleigh, he was soon able to save the money to buy one himself, complete with T-square, compasses, an overhead light, and even a green eyeshade visor. His motto was, "if you're going to do something, jump in with both feet." He sat at the table studying his papers and drawing his latest design.

"Say cheese!" a voice from the door behind him chimed in. He looked over his shoulder at the flash of Rick's new camera.

"How long have you had that?" James asked his oldest brother.

"Oh, I bought it a few months ago."

James turned back to his table. "Look at this new model of the F-14 Tomcat I just bought." He picked up the box of plastic model parts that was sitting on his drafting table. "It's a Navy fighter, the kind they land on aircraft carriers." He turned the box over, explaining the different decals to the brother he hadn't known as well as his middle brother, having been born eleven years apart.

"Looks interesting," Rick said.

"Yeah, and when it's finished, the wings will move back and forth—just like they do when the real ones fly. The skull and cross-bones decal goes on the tail. That's one of the Navy fighters' insignias. They're called...oh, what is it? Something like—oh yeah, here it is: the Jolly Roger. These guys are some of the top pilots in the military."

"Why don't you let me take some pictures of you at your drafting table."

"Sure," he said, not caring one way or the other. "I'm drawing the floor plan to a castle right now. I'll work on that." After a few seconds of looking studious, he turned to Rick: "You know, I've decided to become an architect when I get older." He worked away for five or ten seconds while Rick snapped a few shots.

"Hey, Rick, look at this. It's great. My castle has a dungeon right here," he said, pointing to his drawings. "And the great hall is over here. That's where the king has feasts and parties."

"And where is the vault? The place you keep all the gold to pay for the castle," Rick asked.

"I haven't thought about that." He paused. "That's okay; I can change it. That's the great thing about creating stuff. You can make it like *you* want it to be, can't you?"

Rick continued with a few more shots. Neither brother said anything for half a minute or so. Suddenly, James stopped working and just stared at the paper in front of him, not really looking at anything but staring straight ahead with a blank expression on his face. Without looking up, he spoke in a voice that betrayed a heart

43

that was less sure of itself.

"Rick, do you think I *can* become an architect when I grow up?"

His oldest brother paused just a second too long: "Well, sure, why not?

CHAPTER 5

———◆———

Rainy Days

The start of the week meant a return to school.

The seventh-grade and eighth-grade students were at lunch, eating in the same section of the cafeteria. Sitting at the end of one table, James pulled out a brown-spotted banana.

"Not again," he said to John. "Mom always says bananas are better for you when they get like this, but I don't like them."

"Why don't you ever eat the lunch they offer here at school?"

"Because the school doesn't make peanut butter and jelly sandwiches," James answered.

Between bites, John changed the subject. "Are you gonna enter the Fine Arts Festival or not, James? You know today is the deadline for signing up. You could play something, even if it's 'Chopsticks.'"

"I don't think 'Chopsticks' would put me in the running to win, even if I did it really well, do you?"

"Probably not," he said on second thought. "It's better than doing nothing, though."

"I don't know. It depends on how I feel, I guess. When does it take place?"

"Not until the spring, April or May. I don't know."

James paused and stared at the table for some time. "Maybe I'll try next year," he said.

• • •

A week later, James and Barbara headed back to the hospital, this time for a longer stay. Dr. Robertson thought it best to begin the heavy dose of chemotherapy with James staying at the hospital so his reactions could be monitored.

After completing the usual paperwork and tests, they were shown to his room. Food was allowed this time, but in this case, that wouldn't be a benefit.

In the afternoon, Dr. Robertson came by to see how his patient was and to explain the treatments to them both.

"James, what we'll be doing is pumping a lot of chemicals into your bloodstream, and hopefully, these chemicals will go right to the bad cells in your neck and head area and stop them from growing. That's the point of this. Do you understand?"

"I think so."

"Of course, the bad part is that there will be side effects. They won't be fun, but we'll help you through those, okay?"

He left his nurse, Sandy, to prep the boy by inserting an intravenous needle into his arm and to arrange the chemical treatments that would hang on a rack by his side. She was the right person for this job. In addition to her attractiveness, her sunny disposition helped to set the boy at ease. She could talk to him in such a way that made him smile, even in the middle of this predicament.

"Mrs. Moody..." Dr. Robertson nodded to her as he walked towards the door. Barbara followed. He spoke so the boy could not hear. "This will be the first week of treatments, but he will come to my office in the following weeks. We'll carry on with this course for several weeks, skipping every other week. Hopefully, he won't have to be in the hospital here longer than just this one week."

"I understand."

"Apart from the severe vomiting that usually follows these treatments, you'll eventually begin to see his hair coming out. First, a few strands will be on his pillow in the morning. But a few days following that, it will start coming out in clumps." He stopped for a second. "I just want you to be prepared for this. It won't be a pleasant thing to watch. Okay?"

Barbara nodded.

"You'll also need to be very careful about allowing other people to come around him during these treatments, especially if they have colds or are sick in any way. When these treatments kick in, his immune system will be compromised. He'll be prone to pick up germs or bugs very easily, and that would not be good."

She steeled herself for the coming hours.

"I know this is difficult. Is there someone else from your family who'll be here?"

"Yes, my mother will be coming soon. And I'm sure my husband will stop by after work as well."

Dr. Robertson walked back into the room as Sandy had already inserted the needle and hung the bags of clear liquid on a rod attached to the dispenser. The cold chill of the liquid once again began to course through the boy's body as one chemical after another was slowly pumped in. An odd taste came into his mouth, and he began to feel woozy. About an hour later, the first course had been administered, and he lay in his bed, not feeling well at all. It didn't take long before the urge to throw up came, and it came strong for most of the rest of the day.

Hours later, he lay there completely exhausted, his mother doing all she could to wipe his forehead and help with the disposal.

Each day saw the same procedure, with the same inevitable results. By the end of the week, he was discharged from the hospital but had no ability to walk out on his own this time. The orderly wheeled him to the car waiting at the front of the door, where he got into the back seat and lay down.

• • •

Though the next week was without treatment, he was not able to return to school. Some of his teachers had prepared work for him to do in periods he had the strength to do it so that he could keep up with his classmates. He tackled some of it when he felt up to the job, but mostly, he just lay in his bed.

• • •

The following week saw the process start all over, but this time in Dr. Robertson's office.

"Hi, James," said Sandy with a vivid smile on her face. "Are you ready to let me stick you in the arm again?"

"Well, if you *have* to," he answered with as much humor as he could muster.

"Don't worry. This will be a lot easier than when we started last time. And just think, you get me to talk to as well!"

• • •

Friday came, and the end of another week. He hadn't much energy left but plodded through. Sandy was as cheerful as ever and provided at least one delightful aspect he could look forward to in this whole routine.

After returning home, his mother helped him straight to bed, where he'd lay until the vomiting began again.

Steve came home from his paper route. His mother was in the kitchen, rinsing out rags and buckets and trying to keep an eye on the dinner that simmered on top of the stove. The sound of dry heaves came from James' room just beyond the kitchen. There was nothing left on his stomach to empty, but it didn't stop the reaction from coming.

"Mom, I need to get your signature for this field trip."

She was torn between tasks and didn't hear him. "What? Steve, have you done your homework yet?"

"No, Mom, I just got in. I'll do it later. I need you to sign this for me."

"No, you need to do your homework. We'll be having dinner soon, and your dad will be coming home in about half an hour." She was completely oblivious to the paper he waved in front of her.

"Fine, but could you just sign—"

"Look! I don't have time for this right now. Can't you hear your brother in there? I'm busy. I'll get to it later."

He put the paper back into his backpack and headed to his own room, where he slammed the door shut. Soon after, the sounds of Nerf basketball could be heard coming from the room—the jumping, the backboard shots, and the frustrations.

Half an hour later, Charles came in the back door. The usual sounds of a closing door and deadbolt lock could be heard, after which he walked into the kitchen to greet his wife.

James had calmed down some by this time. He lay quietly, dozing in and out as the family finished their dinner. Steve left after finishing his to return to his homework (and Nerf ball game).

"So, how's he doing, Bobbie?" Charles asked.

"He's had another rough day. But what days *aren't* rough now?"

"How much longer are these treatments going to last?"

"Well, this will be another four to five weeks, and then he goes into radiotherapy." Barbara took a bite of the chicken she had prepared. "Honey, one thing worries me. We're starting to get these medical bills in now—I mean the really big ones. They seem to be coming from every direction right now. Without insurance, I don't know how we're ever going to be able to—"

"Don't!" Charles said in a forceful voice. He stopped her before she could finish. "Don't talk about that. That's none of your business. It's not for you to figure out. You just tell the doctors to do what they have to do. I'll worry about that."

"I do, I do. But how are you going to..."

"What did I say? You look after *him*." He pointed towards James' room. "Make sure he gets what he needs. I'll take care of the bills."

She looked at him and said nothing.

"And don't ever, ever tell the boy about this. Understand? He doesn't need to know about this stuff. We'll make it somehow."

The two embraced for a few seconds. Barbara started to take plates to the sink and continued to clean up the kitchen.

Charles stood up to retreat into his den. Before leaving the kitchen, he filled his coffee cup again while Barbara carried on with post-dinner chores. He left to go to the den but stopped in James' room on his way.

The boy was half-awake as his dad came in.

"Hey there, Jim. I hear you've had a rough day?"

The boy said nothing but nodded his head.

The father placed his cup on a table nearby, kneeled down beside the bed, and placed his hand on the boy's forehead. Even though he worked as an airplane mechanic in the Marine Corps, years of barbering had left him with softer hands than he once had. He spoke quietly and stroked the boy's hair back.

"You just hang in there, kiddo. You can't throw up *all* the time, you know. It'll stop sometime."

The radio sitting on the window sill next to the bed was turned on, but it was so low neither one could hear what was playing on it.

"Here, let me turn the radio up for you a little bit so you can hear. Maybe it will help you get to sleep." He reached over the boy and turned the volume up slightly. Standing back up, he patted the boy on the shoulder. "You get some sleep, okay?"

He shut the door to the bedroom, which sat next to his den, sat down in his armchair, and turned on the television to the nightly news. He took the cup, looked at it for a few seconds, and then drank it. He sat in the chair with his eyes closed, the chaos from the TV blaring, but he didn't really hear what was going on. Soon, he was fast asleep. Barbara put down the dishes she was washing, walked into the living room, closed the door, and got down on her knees as the tears fell from her face.

Back in James' room, the voice of Karen Carpenter played over the radio as he dozed. "Rainy days and Mondays always get me down..."

CHAPTER 6

——◆——

Tender Mercies

In his class at school, John sat next to an empty chair. The late bell had just rung, and Mr. Crane stood in the front of the class.

"Why don't we start this morning by saying a prayer for James? I think all of you know he hasn't been here for sometime because he's been going through some illness. He's having a rough go of it with all of the treatment he's been having. I spoke to his mother yesterday, and she said he probably wouldn't be back to school for many weeks. Let's ask God to help him and his family through this time. It's rough on all of them. But we know that God can help them."

He bowed his head. Those in the class followed his lead.

• • •

As James' strength waxed and waned, he was able to tackle little bits of Math or Science at home. But those were not his favorite subjects. Since he was young, he had learned to love books and stories. In his carefree days, he enjoyed the nights of staying with his grandparents and having his grandmother snuggle in bed with him to read *The City Mouse and the Country Mouse*. As he grew older, the discipline of plodding through the classics in English class unlocked for him the great rewards that came from such a task. It became his preferred subject, and it was always the class he looked forward to the most. Through reading, he began to discover many other worlds and adventures.

Now, at home and away from school for days without end, he began to retreat into the worlds created by others laid out before him on paper. It soon became his primary form of interaction with other people—characters imagined by Charles Dickens, C. S. Lewis, and Mark Twain.

One morning, as he sat in the swing in the backyard reading, Barbara passed by his bed and noticed the covers on his bed turned down. She naturally reached down to straighten the blankets and fluff the pillow but stopped after picking up the pillow. She looked more closely to find several strands of long hair on the pillow cover. She paused, brushed them away, and put the pillow back on the bed, realizing what was to come.

Within the week, the boy's hair began to come out quickly. One evening, she convinced him to just let her brush it all out rather than wait for it all to fall out on its own in clumps. She cried as she did but held back from letting him see her. Afterward, she brought him a small English cap she had picked up at JC Penney for this inevitable sad day and showed it to him.

"How about this, James? You could wear this for now until your hair comes back."

"I don't know," he said, growing very unsure about being out in public.

"Come on. I know it's not the best, but you don't want to wear a wig, do you? I think that would be a little more obvious. At least with this, nobody can see everything underneath."

"Well, I guess so." He let her put it on his head. Inside of himself, though, he dreaded facing the world outside. He knew the way he looked.

With the chemotherapy also came other side effects: the skin turning a sickly pale color and a general appearance of sickliness. With all the nausea and vomiting that followed treatments, he could hardly bear to keep down much food, causing him to lose a lot of weight. By this time, he was not an attractive sight. Thin, pale, hairless, and weak, he was something that would attract attention for all the *wrong* reasons. Nevertheless, he occasionally ventured out into public, but not often. Mostly, those times were in places where there were not many people.

One Saturday morning, the boys were in the den watching weekend cartoons. Bugs was running away from Elmer Fudd, and Wyle E. Coyote was falling off yet another cliff. Barbara stuck her head in the room and told the boys to get washed and ready to go; they were heading out to the mall.

"You guys brush your teeth. We're going out to North Hills shortly. I need to go to Penney's for some bedsheets."

"Can I get another airplane model at the hobby shop?" James asked.

She paused for a few seconds. "Oh, I guess so, as long as it isn't too expensive."

She disappeared into her bathroom to finish dressing and "making her face." No southern woman would be caught dead outside the house without going through that ritual of face-making, of course.

The boys hadn't budged, as Wyle E.'s new supply of dynamite from the Acme company had just arrived.

"Boys! Get ready. *Now*, I said," came a voice from the bathroom. No one moved. But the third time was the charm: "*Now!*"

Steve and James jumped from their places and scurried to their rooms to get dressed.

The boys were ready shortly afterward, and the fifteen-minute drive to the mall was a quiet one. After going inside the main entrance and stopping there, Barbara gave her two sons instructions.

"You boys stay together. I'm going down to JC Penney, where they have curtains and bedspreads. We'll meet together at 1:30 at Chick-fil-A, okay?"

"All right, Mom."

They both made their way to the Hobby Shop, a boy's paradise of models, trains, crafts, and all kinds of mechanical things. Steve made his way to the remote-controlled airplane section. James headed back to look at the plastic model kits. This time he was looking for a model of an aircraft carrier. After finding one he liked, he looked at the price and quickly put it back on the shelf.

She'd never let me get that one. That's too big, he said to himself.

He kept searching for a smaller one with a smaller price.

While scanning the shelves, he started to hear the giggling of some girls on another aisle. *That's an annoying silliness, louder than girls in a public place usually make*, he thought.

I wonder what's so funny, he thought to himself.

He ignored the sounds and kept looking at smaller models, but the childish laughing didn't stop. He looked in the direction of the noise but saw no one else in the aisle. Then, briefly, at the end of the aisle, he could see two heads poking around the shelves looking down his direction. There was no one else *on* his aisle. He ignored them for a few seconds and looked back to the myriad of models before him. At least, he looked in the direction of those many models. But his mind could not focus anymore on what was there. A fear had grabbed hold of him. He stared straight ahead, wondering what course of action he should take. Should he just keep looking and ignore them, or should he try to go somewhere? He had tried to ignore his own appearance when going out, and he tried not to think about what others might think of him. But it couldn't be avoided on some occasions.

Soon the girls, about his age, had ceased hiding behind the shelves and were standing openly at the end of the aisle looking at him, pointing and laughing. They weren't hiding their mockery now. They just stood there arrogantly, demeaning expressions on their faces. Their disgust changed into surprise, curiosity, and incredulity over a short period.

James turned his back to them, pulled his cap down lower on

his head, and closed his eyes. He walked the opposite direction down the aisle, away from the girls and up the other side.

As he walked quickly past the toy trains, he could hear one of the girls say, "What a weirdo." The girls walked away, back to tell their parents about the strange boy they saw.

James headed for the front of the store and out the door. As he walked through the mall, he kept his head down, making sure not to look at anyone around him. He quickened his pace and headed for the JC Penney department store. Once inside, he searched frantically all over the store for his mother. His pace was quick, and he only looked up when he had to, scanning the store without ever making eye contact with anyone. Finally, he found his mother looking at new pillowcases.

"Mom, take me home!" he said urgently.

"James, what is it? I'll be finished in just a minute."

"I have to go home, now. Please, take me home!"

"No. We're going to stay here and have lunch."

"I don't want to be here anymore. I want to go home."

"Wait a few more minutes. I'm nearly done here. Besides, I thought you were looking for a model. And where's your brother?"

"I don't know. He's back at the store, I guess. But I have to leave, Mom. Please!"

Exasperated, she put the package down and started to leave.

"I don't know what's wrong and why you need to leave now.

Are you feeling well?"

"No, I'm not," he answered.

"Well, let's get your brother, and we'll go."

The three of them arrived back at home—no packages to carry inside and no lunch in their stomachs.

"Well, that was a wasted trip," Steve said. He grabbed his bike. "I'm going over to Doug's house to see if he wants to go riding," he told his mom. He rode off up the alley.

James went straight to the back porch, through the door, into his room, and shut the bedroom door behind him. He lay down on his bed, his hat still covering his bald head. And he said nothing more about the day.

• • •

In a few days, the front doorbell rang. It was morning. Steve was at school, Charles was at work. James and Barbara were at the house. Barbara answered the door.

"Hi, are you Mrs. Moody?"

"Yes."

"My name is Kevin Starr. A friend of yours sent me to see you after telling me about your son's illness."

Barbara, not wanting to seem inhospitable, and recognizing the name he mentioned, invited the young man into the house. In fact, the name of the acquaintance was a trusted leader in the community, so her defenses were somewhat lowered. She showed him into the living room, by way of the French doors, and offered him a seat. James came in to see what the commotion was about.

"Do you mind if I wash my hands before I sit down, Mrs. Moody?"

"No, not at all. The bathroom is right through here."

Still unsure, puzzled, and intrigued, she explained to James who sent the man to their house. What his mission was about, exactly, they had no clue. They didn't have to wait long. He returned to the living room and sat down on the sofa next to James.

"Mrs. Moody, I was sent here to heal your son," the man said.

Barbara's eyes widened. "Are you *sure* you were sent by our friend?" she asked suspiciously.

"Yes, he told me about James' cancer and suggested I come down here to heal him. I have that gift, and all I'll have to do is to lay my hands on his neck where the cancer is, and then—"

Barbara cut him short, "Lay your hands on..."

The man reached out and started to place his hands on James' neck, touching him very gently.

"Uh...excuse me, Mr. Starr. Before you do that, can you tell me where you've gotten this gift of healing from?"

"I don't understand. What do you mean?"

"I mean, whose power is this, exactly?"

"Well, it's my power. I have the gift. It's inside of me."

"Really?" Barbara said in unbelief. "So, does the name 'Jesus' mean anything to you?"

"Well, sure. I know He was a healer, too, a man who lived a long time ago. But there are many of us, Mrs. Moody. Healing is something many of us have the power to do. Jesus isn't here anymore. I am."

Barbara ended the conversation abruptly. "Let me show you the door, Mr. Starr. Thank you for your concern, but I'm afraid it's time for you to leave."

"But, I..." the man was truly amazed at being rebuffed. "Don't you want your son healed?"

"Not by you, Mr. Starr." She opened the door and stepped back for him. "Goodbye."

He left, walked outside, and stood on the front porch for a few brief seconds trying to adjust his sense of self-worth after such a rejection. Meantime, Barbara attached the chain lock to the door and walked away.

"What was that all about?" James asked.

"I don't know, but I think I need to have a talk with my 'friend.'"

• • •

Months passed. James was back at school off and on. But his schoolwork never faltered. Through it all, he did the assignments as they were sent home to him. When back at school, he would carry on with his work but made no efforts to speak to others more than he had to.

Over the summer, he turned thirteen. He spent much of his time inside, working on models and drawings. Or, if he was outside, he would be reading while swinging in his favorite place—the only place that let him explore the world without all the risks of interacting with real, live people.

On a hot June afternoon, he sat at his desk, painting the details of the aircraft carrier model his brother had picked up for him on a subsequent trip to the mall, without James.

"James, Jake is here. He wants to know if you want to go outside." Barbara stood at the back door where the friend stood outside. She yelled towards his room. He started to get up from the table where he was working on the model of the ship but stopped just as quickly. He sat there quietly, thinking for one brief moment.

"James? Did you hear me?" his mother repeated.

He looked over at his cap sitting on the desk. He reached out, picked it up, and drew it close to himself. He called back to her.

"I don't feel like going outside today," he said.

"Are you sure you don't want to? The fresh air would be good for you."

"No. I don't." He took the cap and placed it on his head, pulling it down low, and then turned his attention to his model once again.

"I'm sorry, Jake. Maybe he'll feel like it another day," Barbara said to the boy.

He walked away, looking a little puzzled. "Okay, Ms. Barbara.

I'll come back again. Tell him I said hi."

"I'll do that."

Barbara walked into the room. "Are you sure you don't want me to call Jake back? He looked like he really wanted to see you."

"No, I don't feel like it."

"What's wrong? Are you nauseated? Do you have a fever or headache?" She placed her hand on his forehead.

"No."

"Well, what is it, then?"

"I don't know. I just don't want to go out."

She placed her hand on his shoulder. He carried on washing the paint from one of his detail brushes and started to dry it off. She walked away, looking concerned but helpless.

• • •

Charles came home from work, arriving around six-thirty. Steve and Barbara were in the kitchen. Steve was throwing his Nerf basketball at the hoop, which he placed at the kitchen door.

"You'll never guess who came into the shop today," Charles said casually.

"Who?" Barbara asked.

"No, you have to guess."

"Was it Jimmy V?" Steve asked.

"Nope. Afraid not."

"I don't know," Barbara said. "I'm sure I can't guess."

"Agents from the Secret Service," Charles answered dryly.

"The what?" she said. They both looked at him, stunned.

"Yeah. They came to check me out, to see if I was okay, I guess."

"Why you?" Steve asked.

"Because I called the White House. President Reagan is coming to Raleigh to give a speech in a couple of weeks. He'll be right downtown, just a mile or two away, so I called to see if he would come by to visit James. I guess the agents came to see if I was legit or just some crackpot!"

"He's not coming, is he?" Barbara asked.

"No, I don't think so. But it was worth a try."

"I do have a customer, though, who knows one of the senators in the General Assembly. I think he's going to set up a time for James to meet him if he wants. You know how he's really interested in government; well, I thought this might cheer him up."

And as quickly as he came in the door, the mood of the room changed.

Charles walked over to the coffeepot to pour his nightly dose of caffeine before heading to the den.

• • •

It was not long before his dad's connections in the political world came through for him. James received a letter in the mail inviting him to go to the General Assembly building in downtown Raleigh to meet Senator Blake, a friend of one of the men who got his haircuts from Charles. The legislators were in session at the time, and he would also be free to sit in the gallery to watch the proceedings.

The evening arrived. He put on his red and blue striped tie, blue blazer and khaki trousers, and of course, the cap which he wore everywhere. He walked the ten or fifteen minutes it took him to get there, just five or six blocks from their home in the Oakwood neighborhood. Showing his letter to the receptionist, she directed him to the right wing of the building, where he found the senator's office.

"You must be James," the senator said as his secretary showed the boy into the office. "Sit down, sit down." He pointed to a chair in front of his desk.

The senator was cordial and kind. He explained the procedures of making laws for the state and gave him a lapel pin in the shape of the state of North Carolina.

"So, are you interested in public service, James?"

"I don't know. Maybe. But you have to give a lot of speeches, don't you?"

"Well, yes, talking does come with the job. That's how we *try* to persuade others to agree with us on what laws to pass. Of course, doing the right thing is the most important part; you know, helping people of the state."

"Do you?"

"Do we what?"

"Do you help a lot of people?"

"Well," the senator looked away briefly, "let's hope so." He gave a timid smile. "Listen, our session is going to be called to order in about fifteen minutes, James. So, why don't you go up into the gallery, and you can watch what happens from there."

"Okay."

"I'm afraid that what's on the agenda is not all that interesting tonight, but at least you'll get to see how we do things."

They walked into the hallway together, shook hands, smiled, and went opposite directions.

James made his way up the red-carpeted stairs to the third floor, overlooking both the house chamber and the senate chamber. No one was in either one of the galleries, except maybe one or two stray reporters. It obviously was a boring agenda. Nevertheless, he opened one of the glass doors and walked down to the very front aisle of the balcony.

Nothing was really happening yet. A few legislators wandered around, waiting for the gavel to come down. Some assistants carried stacks of paper, doling out clipped packets to each senator's desk. Not long after, before the session began, a man entered through the same door behind James and walked down to him.

"I'm sorry, young man, you're going to have to remove your hat in here." He wore a dark suit with a name tag on it. He was the Sergeant-at-Arms.

James wasn't sure what to say. "Oh...but...but you see, I have..."

"It's one of the rules of the chamber. There are no exceptions. You'll have to take it off."

"But...but I can't...because I don't..."

The officer of order and decorum did not give him a chance to answer. "You *have* to take it off, young man; otherwise, you'll have to leave the chamber." His manner was brusque and impatient. He wasn't waiting for an explanation, and James sensed that nothing he could say would convince the man to let him keep the cap on. But he wasn't going to take it off either. He'd never been in public showing his hairless head, and he hadn't the boldness to do it now. He took the only course that came to his mind—retreat.

He stood up and left, the Sergeant-at-Arms holding the door open for him. He walked down the red-carpeted stairs quickly and out into the summer night air. At the entrance to the building, two tall flagpoles with one enormous flag on each one fluttered in the wind. The twenty-eight-foot great seal of the state, set in marble and granite on the walkway, was lit up by the surrounding lights. The state's motto, written in Latin, stood out in large brass letters around its edge: "To be rather than to seem." It was the first thing people saw as they walked to the front of the building.

James passed it quickly, keeping his head down and hat down even further. He kept walking straight across the street and up the plaza to the old capitol building, lit up from every angle as the sky began to darken. He slowed his pace once he stepped onto Capitol Square. Almost no one was there.

This was a place he had ridden his bike many times before the disease. It was his hangout, the place of adventure, the great "downtown" in which were found so many curiosities, oddities, and old things. The stillness of the old capitol building calmed him a little after the frustration of having to leave the General Assembly building. He walked around to the east side, looking at the main statue of three presidents born in North Carolina. He walked to the west side and looked up at the memorial to the Confederate soldiers—men and boys—who had died defending their homes. He walked past the governor's office, peered through the windows in hopes of seeing someone, but didn't. He stopped on the south side and looked up at the statue of George Washington, flanked by two Revolutionary War cannons. Above the revered General rose the capitol dome itself and the American flag, fluttering only slightly, but lit up for the whole city to see.

James' eyes became transfixed at the sight. Again his vision focused not on the symbol of his country but on something beyond it that he could not quite grasp but certainly felt. The flag itself blurred in his vision, and the movements he watched were in his mind's eye. He just didn't know what he was feeling, seeing, or sensing. The serenity he had felt once before when he began to "see" this way again overtook him, and an idea again seemed to rise from deep within him in the quiet: "You are to be a seer to my people."

He was startled back to the warm evening by a car horn blaring from Hillsborough Street, still sitting behind another car stopped at one of the traffic lights. Stirring himself, he began moving along his familiar path back to Elm Street.

As soon as he got there, he went into the living room where his mother kept her desk and her books. He searched through the old glass-paned bookcases until he found the Bible dictionary. He placed it on the desk and looked up the word "seer." Surprised to find it listed in the book, he read the definition: "one who speaks for God to man."

James' face grew puzzled. "Speaks for God?" he said out loud. "That's a preacher! I don't want to be a preacher. God, if there's one thing I am not going to do, it's to be a preacher."

He closed the book shut and left the room.

Charles Moody, ca. 1950s

Barbara Newsome (New Bern High School, N.C., mid-1950s)

Reece and Rose Welch, beloved grandparents

Robert (Skinny) Newsome, grandfather

Just starting out—Charles & Barbara

The Cherokee Boys Bluegrass Band (Skinny with mandolin in the middle)

The young family on Elm
Street, early 1970s (James
on left)

James, three years old

James (left) and Stephen (right) with family dogs

Ninth birthday party with first piano (and superheroes)

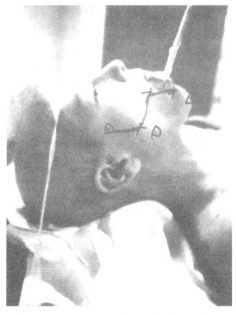

The only photos taken during illness

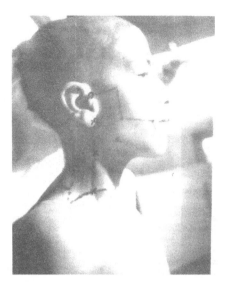

Preparing for radiation treatments

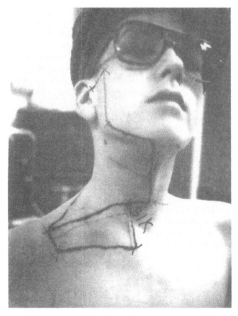

The hat didn't often come off!

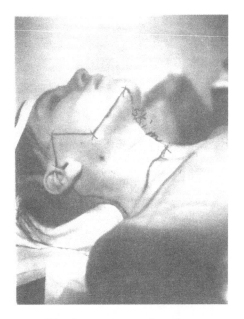

Playing connect-the-dots

High School graduation, age seventeen

Going on the road to share the message of hope

CHAPTER 7

Making Music

Soon, the second stage of treatments for James began—a course of radiation therapy that would last weeks.

Dr. Thompson was the physician overseeing the radiation treatments. They met him in his offices at Rex Hospital on a Monday morning.

"Hello, James," he said as he came into the examination room. "Hello, Mrs. Moody."

"Good morning, Doctor."

"Now, James, I need to explain to you what we're doing here." He was a middle-aged man, his manner not as calm or tranquil as previous doctors they encountered. He was kind, of course, but his was the personality of the doer, the action-man, the solver of problems. He imparted to his patients an assurance of supreme competence, skill, and knowledge. He knew what he was talking about. He leaned forward on his rolling stool.

"In another room just around the hall is a large machine that will send out waves of radiation when it's turned on. When you come in each morning, the technicians will take you in there, lay you on the table where you have to remain perfectly still for the time of treatments..." He made the point by holding his hands spread apart and immovable, "...and they will move the machine around your head until it's in the correct place to release the radiation. That will happen three times, as they release the rays from different angles. Understand?" He was clear, precise, and to the point.

"Yes."

"We'll do this every day, Monday through Friday, for about six weeks. Then we'll have some more scans to see what it looks like inside."

"Doctor, what will the side effects be to this treatment?" Barbara asked.

"I was just about to get to that." He sat back, crossing his arms and straightening up. "He won't actually feel anything when the radiation is released. In time, though, the area we aim the treatment at will become darkened, just like skin does with a suntan. The skin will become tough to the touch, though. On the inside, that's a little harder to determine. The treatment will have an effect on the other organs, apart from where that nasty cancer is we're trying to stop. He'll lose his taste buds for a while, but they should return. And it will weaken his teeth a great deal as well, so you might need to get in touch with your dentist about getting some extra fluoride treatment."

"Will it affect his appetite?"

"Any kind of treatment like this can have negative effects on the body's normal functions. But it shouldn't have too much of a direct bearing on his eating, apart from the taste buds, of course. The area of his neck may be somewhat affected in its normal development too."

"Will you start the treatment today?" James asked.

"No, we'll start that tomorrow. What we need to do today is make sure we have the exact points marked on your face and neck so that each time you come in, the technicians will know exactly where to aim the treatments. What they'll do is mark you with tiny little dots of permanent ink."

"Permanent? You mean, like *forever* permanent?" James asked.

"Yeah," said Dr. Thompson, making it sound not as bad as James had made it sound. "But it'll be only a few little pinpricks. They will hardly be noticeable, James."

The doctor took the boy to the treatment room, where he and the technicians used the laser targeting lights to line up the precise location for the marks. Using a black marker, they outlined the area of his face and neck and proceeded to imprint the key spots on his body with a needle. Every day would be like playing "connect the dots" on his face (as James later told his friends).

For six weeks, he was off school again. Each morning was taken up with the drive to the hospital, the wait in the lobby, and the treatment itself.

About four weeks into the therapy, Barbara stopped the nurse who came to fetch James for the treatment.

"Would it be okay if I came back there with you this morning to see how the treatment is done?"

"Well..." she paused, "... let me go ask the technician in charge if it will be okay. I'll be right back." She took James on into the treatment room and soon came back to the waiting area, motioning to Barbara to follow her.

The room where the massive machine sat was cold and dim. The control panel was complicated and protected behind lead-covered walls. Barbara stood out of the way, watching on a closed-circuit TV screen as the technicians made their preparations: connecting the dots, rotating the giant arms of the apparatus, and finally, placing a popsicle stick wrapped with surgical tape into James' mouth. It had been rigged for use in order for him to hold his mouth open at the right angle for them to get the exact exposure they needed.

Holding that stick in his mouth was the worst and most trying part of the ordeal: lying on the table with his head back, throat open, and an object the size of a balled-up sock down his throat; he was unable to swallow and had to remain perfectly still.

Barbara looked at her son: a thirteen-year-old boy who wasn't big before the first of the treatments. He now appeared as just skin and bones. The treatments had affected his appetite, and he didn't succeed much in eating a lot of food or keeping much down. The sickly color of his skin gave him the appearance of a ghost. She stayed, watching the process through the first course of the day, but she could not remain. When the technicians entered to make adjustments to the patient, she left the room quietly, in tears. She went out to her car to be alone.

As soon as she had settled him in his bed back at home, she shut herself into her bathroom, once again lying face down on the carpet, once again turning to the only One she knew who could help.

By the end of the six weeks, the boy's outward appearance certainly was nothing to gaze at but was, rather, something that would make one want to turn away. But inwardly, as the doctors reported, the treatments were helping. Things were looking good. Things were looking much better. All the scans showed no sign of the cancer that had first appeared as a lump on his neck. Conferences with Dr. Robertson and Dr. Thompson resulted in the cessation of any kind of further treatment for the time being. James would have time to recover physically from the effects of the treatments themselves.

And in his recovery, along with his books, his piano also became a place of retreat.

Since becoming ill, piano lessons had to go by the wayside. He had managed to complete a few years before this ordeal. But his music did not get put on a shelf. He began to improvise. He began to pick out tunes by ear. He began to copy sounds he heard from other pianists and tried to imitate their styles.

One afternoon, while sitting at the old upright piano putting chords together, picking out melodies, and playing musical phrases over and over again, his mother called out from the kitchen.

"James, how about we go up to Granddaddy's house this weekend?" Barbara asked.

"Sure. Okay," he answered.

"He asked for you to bring the little electric keyboard you got at the flea market. Maybe you two could play something together."

"Mom, I can't play like that. I can put chords together, but I can't just play the piano if I don't know a song."

"Sure you can. He'll show you a few things, I'm sure. After all, where do you think you got that talent from? It wasn't your father or me. It was your granddaddy Skinny!"

She was right. His grandpa, her biological father, was the only musical one in the family that anybody could find. It *had* to be him.

Friday came along with lots of afternoon traffic leaving town, which they mostly avoided by leaving before the big rush hour. The one-and-a-half-hour drive to Roanoke Rapids took them along some country roads, through the small towns of Rolesville, Louisburg, and Centerville (the last crossroads being his favorite place to stop because of the one gas station's bars of colored coconut striped candy: pink, white, and brown). In fact, that was about all there was in Centerville, except a few houses dotted around the area.

They arrived in Roanoke Rapids just before dinner time, coming up the back way on State Highway Forty-eight. They passed by the now disused train station and crossed over the railroad tracks to get to the old mill houses where Barbara had grown up.

Each street hosted the same kinds of houses, all built to service the workers of the mills that once provided the engine of the community. Most of the mills were now shut, but at least one was still operating, as anyone driving within twenty miles of it could tell, given the stink of sulfur coming out of the smokestacks.

They drove down Rapids Street and parked near the intersection of West Tenth Street.

"Bobbie, when was the last time you changed the oil on that car?" her father asked as they got out of the car. He was waiting on the front porch.

"Oh, just last month, Daddy. Don't worry. I haven't forgotten that part of my childhood training: *If you want to keep your car running for a long time, change the oil regularly.*"

Apart from being a car enthusiast (as evidenced by the 1962 Chevelle in the driveway), the sixty-five-year-old man worked much of his later life as a service station attendant (in the days when attendants actually *attended* to customers and serviced their cars). In his younger family days, he—like so many others—worked at the mills nearby.

"Come on, boy," he called out to James. "After we eat something, we'll go upstairs to my studio and make some music. Leave that keyboard in the trunk until later. We'll get it on the way up!"

They sat around the old table in the house that looked just like every other kitchen in every other house on the street and talked of recent news, family gossip, and local friends.

"I heard he moved up to Garysburg," Skinny said.

"Well, that's what she told *me*, Daddy. I don't know."

James finished as much of his small pork chop and cornbread he could and took his plate to the sink.

"I'm going outside to the swing for a little bit," he said.

"All right, but as soon as Dooley gets here, we're gonna go up to the studio!"

James went outside to sit in the swing on the back porch. The others carried on their chatter, and soon the sound of dishes being washed in the sink tumbled out the back door. Five minutes later, his grandpa came out and sat in the chair beside the swing.

"Your momma tells me you're playing more piano by ear. Is that right?"

"Yes, sir."

"That's good. That's what you need to do." He paused and looked into the small yard where he used to tend to chickens, a pig, and a garden when his own children were growing up. It was now covered over by grass, at least in some patches.

"You know, boy, me and my band the Cherokee Boys used to hitch-hike back in the days when we was young. We played a live radio show every Saturday morning down in Rocky Mount. That was a long drive back then."

James listened but said nothing.

"We practiced a lot in those days because you got to find that perfect sound, *your* sound if you're gonna make music. It ain't just a matter of making an instrument sound pretty. You got to make it sing. Know what I mean?"

The boy timidly nodded his head and kept swinging. He looked at the old apple tree sitting in the middle of the yard, remembering the taste of the ripe and not-so-ripe apples he ate from it in the past.

"Some of those fancy folks can sit down and play every note on a piece of paper if they practice hard enough and learn what to do." He paused. "But to make real music, it ain't gonna come from here." He pointed to his head. "It's got to come from deep inside here," he said, pointing to his chest. The aging man looked away. If the twilight hadn't come so quickly, the boy would have seen a tear appear in the man's eye as he remembered some of the joys of a younger life.

"Why don't we go get that little electronic keyboard of yours and take it upstairs. Let's see what we can do!"

The two walked inside, letting the swinging door slam on their way in. Skinny (an apt nickname that was chosen by his friends early on in life) and his daughter headed up the stairs. James went out the front door to the street where the car was and retrieved his small instrument.

Some of Skinny's other family members were already upstairs. His half brothers Pete and Bahnson were tuning up their banjo and guitar. Dollbaby was sitting in his chair, ready to sing. After five minutes of helping James set up his keyboard and hook it to an amplifier, Skinny took out his mandolin, guitar, and harmonica. He placed his bass drum at a right angle for his foot. As he played, he would switch instruments as needed or give solos on the harmonica. James followed on the keyboard the best that he could, as his mom and the others sang in simple but elegant Bluegrass harmony.

There's a land that is fairer than day

And by faith we can see it afar

For the Father waits over the way

To prepare us a dwelling place there

In the sweet by and by

We shall meet on that beautiful shore

In the sweet by and by

We shall meet on that beautiful shore[1]

CHAPTER 8

—◆—

Faithful in Small Things

It would be a few more weeks before he could return to school, but when he did, he stopped by the office. He asked for the sign-up sheet for the Fine Arts Festival tryouts. He scanned the list of categories and saw John's name printed under "brass instrumentalists."

"I guess he's gonna give it another shot," he said to himself. After pausing for a few seconds, he looked to see if anyone else was watching and then wrote his name under "Vocalist: Male Solo."

• • •

When James came home that day, he went to his piano. He sat there for half an hour before dinner, trying to pick out a tune by ear, trying to copy sounds he had heard others play. Barbara was in the kitchen next to the living room, cooking dinner and talking on the phone.

"Oh yes, Pansy. I forgot to tell him. Hold on a minute, let me get him," she said.

"James! Come here a minute." He walked in, impatient at being interrupted. "Did I tell you what your aunt said to me a few months ago?" She stopped talking to him, having been interrupted by the voice on the phone. "Okay, okay. I'm sorry," she said into the mouthpiece. She turned to the boy: "It was last year she said this about your music. Did I tell you?"

"Tell me what?" The boy was thoroughly confused by now.

"Did I tell you that your aunt felt very strongly that God wants you to sing?"

"What?"

"Sing! You know, while playing the piano—sing *and* play the piano—together."

"No, you didn't tell me that."

"Well, she did! And now I've told you. So go off and do it!" She waved him back into the living room. Her conversation returned to the voice on the phone. "Well, I forgot. I've got so many things on my mind right now, Pansy." She then changed the conversation entirely.

James returned to the piano stool again. *Sing? Sing* and *play?* It was all he could do to figure out how to play a song he'd never learned by music, much less try to sing as well.

At dinner time, Charles came through the back door, and Barbara called the boys to come into the kitchen to eat. They were all sitting down together (except for the times Barbara had to get up once again to get something for the meal that she had forgotten). Each time she'd repeat her mother-in-law's rule: *If you don't have it on the table when you start eating, then just leave it.*

"You have a good day, honey?" she asked her husband after they had settled down.

"'Bout average, I guess."

"I had an interesting day."

"That's good."

"Charles, I was talking to a missionary up in Virginia today about a trip they are taking to India."

"Why?"

"Well, I was praying today and began to sense something very strongly about what I need to do."

"Which is?" He was actually paying attention at this point.

"How would it be... I mean... Would you mind if..." She paused and looked at him, letting out a big breath. "Charles, I feel I need to go on this mission trip to India for six weeks. I don't know why, but I feel very strongly about it. I've talked to my sister who's willing to look after everybody here. She'll cook for you and take the boys to school. Would that be okay?"

The boys looked up at her and kept eating. They looked at their father.

"Well, I... I guess so. If this is something you think God wants you to do." He was quiet for a few minutes, then added, "But, you're gonna have to get your own money to pay your way, you know? We can't afford something like this right now."

"I know, I know. God will provide that if it really is something

He wants me to do."

"You'll be gone for six *weeks*?" James asked.

"Yes, James."

"When will you leave?" Steve questioned.

"I think they've planned to leave the middle of next month," she answered.

After the boys had left the kitchen to work on homework, Charles lingered in the kitchen.

"So, Bobbie, you're sure about this trip?"

"Yes, Dear, I think I am. It won't be too hard around here. James is doing fine in school now. He's so much stronger and seems to be settled back in. Steve is doing well too, don't you think?"

"Yeah." He paused a minute as he walked out. "But you're still going to have to find out how to pay for this trip."

Moments later, James came back into the kitchen, where Barbara was still busy washing up.

"What are you going to do in India?" he asked.

"Well, teach the people we meet there, just like we do in church here."

"But why do you have to go over *there*? Can't you do it here?"

"Yes, I can, James, but that's not really the..." Barbara stopped rinsing the plates and turned around to the boy. She decided to explain things in a different way.

"Do you remember the place you use to go for summer camp,

down at Falcon?"

"Yes."

"You know that my grandmother and Papa use to live there. That was Granny's mom and dad. He was a circuit preacher, and they use to live there."

"Yeah, I remember you telling me about that." The boy began to grow slightly agitated and uncomfortable.

"Then you also remember that my grandmother died there from the flu, in the early nineteen hundreds. She was only about forty years old. At the time, your granny was only seven years old."

"I don't really see what this has to do with India."

Barbara resumed her dish-washing. Before your great-grandma died, she called all of her children to her bedside. She put her hands on their heads and prayed for each one of them. Not only that, but she prayed for their children and their grandchildren. That's you and me."

"What did she pray for?"

"She prayed for us to do what God wants us to do." She paused and turned to the boy again. He looked away from her and was clearly agitated. "God wants me to go on this trip. I don't know all the reasons why, but I don't have to know."

Not really hearing an explanation that satisfied him, James left the kitchen and went back to his room. There it was again—preachers. Well, it was something that his family had done in the past, but as for him, he had bigger plans than that for his life, other things he wanted to do in life.

● ● ●

Not long afterward, the second-hand car Charles had bought for Barbara sat in the school parking lot—burning. Not *purposely*, of course. One afternoon, she drove to school to pick up the boys. As soon as she had parked it and turned the engine off, an electrical short under the hood sparked a fire that resulted in melted tires, a visit from the local fire department, lots of excitement around campus, and money left over from the insurance payout that would cover the cost of her upcoming trip to India. For several months it remained one of the highlights of the school year, much to the regret of the Moody brothers.

At the airport, the family gathered at the gate and hugged their mother-missionary goodbye. James looked very unsure. The family had never been parted for such a long time before. He was reluctant to accept this change and hung back. Barbara came over to give him one last hug.

"Don't worry, Son. I'll be home soon. Sometimes, when God wants us to do something for Him, we have to make sacrifices. But you'll see—the time will fly by." She paused a minute. "Do your best on your singing, okay? I wish I could be there to hear you."

He brushed back tears as his mom walked to the plane. They stuck around long enough to see the plane take off for New York, its ultimate destination being Bombay.

The fifteen-minute drive home was quiet.

James spent much time in the backyard, weather permitting, sitting in the swing underneath the oak tree, going back and forth as he read. If not there, he was at his drafting desk in his room or at the piano. Not much else grabbed his attention. For hours he would practice techniques or riffs on the piano he had heard from others. Painstakingly, he would work them out, trying to repeat the same sounds from the recordings he listened to, many times with success, oftentimes with only frustration.

One afternoon he had worked very hard to master a technique. It was still on his mind as he went to bed that night. He could not get the sound out of his head, but he just could not figure out how to repeat it for himself on the keyboard. But that night, he had a remarkable dream. In fact, he dreamed that the pianist whose recording he had been trying to duplicate was there with him, sitting at the piano, showing him how to play that one riff. It was so easy in his sleep. Why did it prove to be so hard when awake?

Getting up the next day, he once again put his mind to the task as he sat down at the tinny-sounding saloon-style piano. To his surprise, the technique he had tried so hard to master simply came out of him and onto the keyboard—no struggle, no effort, no hard work of trying to make his fingers obey his ears. It simply flowed.

It was a glorious sensation. He himself was the one most surprised by the experience. *Maybe there is something inside of me that is useful*, he thought. The feeling was heavenly: here was freedom, emotion, and euphoria. Here was the release of his soul onto the instrument's keys that came from sources he never knew were there. Here was music like his grandpa had described.

And he ventured even further. Though he had sung in the school choir, he had never attempted to sing and play by himself. But the more he stayed at that piano, the greater the feeling to express himself came over him. Soon, the urge within him to voice the words he was hearing became too strong to resist. His efforts were feeble at first—simple melodies, simple phrases. His attempts at combining an improvised piano piece with singing began to drive him and consume his time, his energy. And it was just in the nick of time.

The tryouts for the Fine Arts Festival soon arrived. He would be singing a piece in front of the school's choir director. Just the two of them were in the room, no other audience.

"So, James, what would you like to sing for the competition?"

"It's this." He handed the music to her.

"Okay," she said. "Let's give it a go." She squinted at the score for a couple of seconds and said, "Are you sure this isn't too high for you?"

"No, ma'am, I don't think so."

"That's right. You *are* a counter-tenor, aren't you?"

"I think so." He wasn't sure what a "counter-tenor" was. He only knew that his voice hadn't begun to change yet. Though he was fourteen years old, the extensive course of radiation he had received on his throat would ensure that it never would change as much as it does for most adolescent boys.

She placed her fingers on the keyboard and played the introduction, glancing up at the boy whose shyness and timidity were all too evident. When he missed the cue to begin, she stopped playing.

"Let's try that again, okay? I'll give you a nod when to start."

"Sorry."

She started again, looking up and nodding her head at the right time.

Over in the Land of Promise, a garden sits quiet still...

Outside the closed door to the choir room were five or six other students leaning against the wall. Some were talking with others about their song selections; others were close to the door, straining to hear what was going on inside. Thirty seconds later, the door opened up, and James walked out, holding his music and looking down.

"How'd you do?" Susan asked.

"I don't know," he answered.

"Well, don't worry. We'll all find out pretty soon."

"Yes, I guess we will."

The choir director's voice called out from the room: "Susan! You're next. Come on in."

Three agonizing days later, the finalists were announced in the morning assembly. These winners would face off against the best from many other schools across the state. When James' name was called, he dared not even look around him. He tried to keep his eyes straight ahead on the choir director at the podium or down on the ground in front of him. After it was over, he made his way up to ask her again if she was sure he had gotten through.

"Yes, James. I called your name, didn't I?"

"Yes, ma'am. But I wanted to make sure."

"Don't worry. You'll do fine. You did well in the tryouts, and that's a great song to sing."

The boy started to walk away.

"Oh, James!" she called after him.

He turned around sharply and moved forward to where she stood.

"Just remember: it is a great song, and I'm sure you'll do fine. But to do your best, you've got to sing those words with all of your heart...and mean them. Understand?"

"Yes, Miss Kelly."

CHAPTER 9

———◆———

First Steps

Far away, in a different time zone, on a different continent, Barbara adjusted the sari she was wearing to the meeting that night. Outside of Ahmedabad in the Gujarat region, on the western side of India, she still could not quite get the hang of how to wrap the garment. Washing it in the creek, just like the other women of the area, was a whole other challenge. More than once, it nearly washed away down the stream from her, as she was not able to get hold of it all at once.

Going out the door to walk the few miles to the meeting, one of the leaders of the missionary group with whom she was traveling turned to her.

"I want you to speak at the meeting tonight," said the seasoned and stern companion.

"Me? You mean to the whole crowd?"

"Yes, you. You've spoken to large groups before, haven't you?"

"Well, I've taught a Sunday school class, and I'm happy speaking to people one-on-one, but I've never spoken to a group of hundreds of people."

"You'll do fine."

"But, what do I say to them? I don't know what to say."

"They're hurting, suffering people, Barbara. You tell them about the One who can help them, make them whole, put them back together again. Tell them what He's done in your life."

The missionary was a little terse and not a little impatient with the newcomer. She turned away and quickened her pace to catch up with the rest of the group, who were already heading out.

After an hour's walk, a three-hour meeting, and another hour's walk back to the village, the group returned to the sparse home of their hosts sometime after midnight. Exhausted but exhilarated, Barbara lay down to rest. Her sleep was troubled, though, as unwelcome thoughts crept into her mind.

At six o'clock that morning, she was awakened by a gentle knocking at the door. Not wanting to disturb the others who were sleeping on the floor nearby and being the first one to awake, she roused herself, went over to the door, and opened it up. A small Indian girl, nine or ten years of age, stood with a face full of longing.

"You come," she said to the mother, motioning with her hand.

The girl began to walk away but looked back and continued to urge Barbara to follow. She knew the girl, a member of the family with whom she was staying.

Not knowing what the disturbance was about, Barbara put her sandals on and quietly made her way to the direction the girl had walked. She soon reached the front door of the house, which stood wide open. The morning's rays were already beginning to illuminate the new day, and the light poured in through the opening. She crossed the threshold to see a sight that broke her heart.

There in front of the house were children of all ages, from four to thirteen, all dressed for school. Ten or fifteen of them stood in a line, at the head of which stood the young girl who knocked on the door to rouse her. Barbara walked over to her and placed her hand on the girl's head.

"What is all this, Susanna? Why are these children here?"

The girl looked up at her, put her hands together, and said, "You pray? You will please pray for us?"

Barbara struggled to hold back the tears as she smiled at the simple faith of the girl.

"Yes, I will pray for you," she said and knelt down to do the work she had been called there to do.

When the last child had left, she sat there watching them go on their way, waving goodbye as they headed to their classes for the day.

As her thoughts naturally turned to her own family and home, a strong impression gripped her heart. Though the day was growing to be hot and dry, an apprehension seemed to come down over her in the same way the thunder clouds creep up on a hot August afternoon back in the Carolinas. She once again began to feel a heaviness in her soul for her own loved ones back at home, and specifically for her youngest son, James. She dropped her head down in prayer, but this time it was not for the children of India.

In little more than a whisper, the words dropped from her lips: "No, God. Not again..."

• • •

It was Sunday afternoon, and Charles was in the backyard. Since time immemorial, his favorite car was the Cadillac, and as on many other Sundays when the weather was fine, he was under the hood of his present Sedan de Ville, a twenty-five-year-old model with the iconic old-style Batmobile fins on the back. Whether it needed any repair work or not was really not the point of being there most of the time. It was the tinkering that held his interest—always looking for a way to save money by doing his own maintenance and work and an excuse to get out of his den and under a car hood.

Steve was outside practicing his golf swings since he'd recently joined the school's golf team. James came out with nothing specific in mind but just to see what the others were doing. He walked over to his dad, who was leaning over the engine.

"Go turn the key, Jim, until I say stop."

The boy obeyed excitedly. He turned it over...*click, click, click.* Nothing else happened.

"All right, all right," Charles called out, exasperated by now. "Turn it back, all the way back."

James got out and came to the front of the car. "What's wrong with it?" he asked.

"Well, that's what I'm *trying* to find out. I don't know if this thing needs a new battery or a new starter. Let's hope it's just the battery."

"Is it a big job to replace the starter?"

"Yeah, well, at least it'll cost a lot more money. Pop the trunk and get the jumper cables. I'll pull your mom's car over here to see if we can jump it off her battery."

Despite her car having burned up at the school, Barbara had managed to pay for the trip to India with the insurance money and had a few hundred dollars left over with which she bought her pastor's very old Chevrolet Impala.

"Can I drive it over?" Steve yelled from across the yard.

"Okay. But be careful. Drive it slow."

After a few false starts and riding the brake all the way over to the Cadillac, he parked it just in front of Charles' car. Their father proceeded to connect the jumper cables, the boys watching to remind themselves of how the operation was to be done.

"There we go," said Charles. "Okay, Jim, start it up now."

James turned the key, and the engine started straight away. He revved the engine up just a little bit.

"Not too much!" Charles yelled above the engine's noise. "Just let it sit for a few minutes."

Steve had returned to his improvised pitch and putt course in the backyard. James and Charles stood near the open hood, watching the various parts of the engine work together as they were intended.

"All it needed was a little current to start it right up," Charles explained knowingly. He stepped back and wiped his greasy hands on an old rag. "No current, no ignition. That's how it works." He looked at his youngest son briefly. The two remained silent for a minute, just looking at the car. Finally, James spoke.

"Dad, you know that story on the news last night we saw about the kids in Ireland?"

"What story is that?"

"About the violence in Ireland where guys are getting killed and leaving their sons without fathers?"

"Oh yeah, I remember."

"Well, how can it go on? Why doesn't somebody do something to stop it?"

His dad gave a deep sigh before venturing an answer. "Well... you're right. It is terrible. But I guess some people are just too busy with their own lives, just trying to get by, to go out and stop it. Other people just can't deal with it, I guess. They try to find ways to block it out of their mind. That's one reason some people start..." His voice tapered off, and he turned his attention back to the car. After a couple of minutes of tinkering, he stood up again.

"You ready for your singing contest coming up?"

"I think so. I'm not sure I can do it all by memory, but I'm still practicing it."

"Good, good," his father encouraged. "Practice makes perfect. And don't forget your syncopation." He looked at the boy and shook his pointing finger back and forth.

James rolled his eyes, smiled, and decided to retreat back into the house before his father started the lecture on musical technique again.

He went back in, sat down on the sofa in his father's den, and turned on the television. He picked up a copy of *Time* magazine. From the front cover stared back a young Irish boy, ten or eleven years old. On the boy's face was a blank, grieved expression. James flipped through the pages to find the story about this boy. He saw other children—all victims of the troubles (so they called the problems in Northern Ireland at the time)—all children who no longer had fathers to protect them. His heart broke while looking at the forlorn faces.

"Why doesn't somebody *do* something," he said to himself.

He put the magazine down and picked up the TV remote. After a few seconds of quickly flipping through channels, a black and white image flashed across the screen. He stopped and reversed course (being partial to older films).

On the screen was an English actor dressed in an academic gown. He was talking to an ordinary-looking boy by the name of Tom who was adjusting to his first days at the famed boarding school in England called Rugby. As James would later discover, the film was an old version of Thomas Hughes' English novel, *Tom Brown's School Days*.

But this was the first time James had ever come across the story. And from the start, there was something in it that gripped him. He didn't know what it was in this story that so held his attention. All he knew was an excitement and a yearning within himself. It was like a hunger that was being fed, a desire that was being satisfied, a longing that was being fulfilled. He sat there, glued to the television, drinking in every word, gesture, image, and accent.

A thought rose up in his mind: *One day, you'll be there.*

He sat watching it and taking in every detail, hoping the film would not end too soon.

• • •

The day for the Fine Arts Festival had come. It took place on a Saturday and would last the whole day. Buses from schools across the state filled the parking lot of Wake Christian Academy in Raleigh. The campus resembled an ant colony with scores of people moving in all different directions. Instruments were being moved, adjusted, and moved again to make room for new contestants; works of art were displayed on every available wall; classrooms served as assembly points where contestants for specific categories would cluster to find out *where* they should be, *when* they should be, and *what* exactly they would be doing *before* their scheduled slots arrived. Teachers and students of the school served as volunteers guiding traffic (both in and outside the buildings), tour guides, messengers, and all-around founts of knowledge about the day's events.

"I don't know if I can do this," James said to John.

"*You* don't know?" he answered. "I can't find the mouthpiece to my trombone. How am I supposed to play like *that*?"

The two shook their heads more with nervousness than with excitement.

The morning moved on quickly. At lunchtime, the winners of the visual arts categories were announced after the judges had spent the morning looking at pen and ink drawings, watercolor paintings, chalk drawings, clay sculptures, and an infinite number of other works of art that could be categorized. Instrumental solos took place after lunch and, finally, the vocalists.

John's jazz rendition of "When the Saints Go Marching In" on the trombone was performed without flaw thanks to his well-prepared mother who found the mouthpiece for him. He walked off the stage and sat next to James.

"Good job," James remarked. "I didn't think you were going to pull off that last note, but you always did have lots of hot air!"

John looked over to him and stuck his tongue out like a dog panting. He said, "Yeah, and it's all gone *now*."

An hour later, the next to last male vocalist walked off the stage. James was the last one out of four, not the best position for a contestant. Now he had to do better than everyone he had just heard, and the standard had been set pretty high.

He walked up onto the stage. His choir director, Miss Kelly, had settled in at the piano. He announced the name of the song in a nervous voice.

"I'm going to sing..."

"Sorry! Can you speak a little louder, please?" said one of the judges, cupping his ear to his hand.

James cleared his throat, looked down, and took a big breath.

"I'm going to sing a song called 'Gethsemane.'"

"Thank you," the judge responded.

He looked over at his accompanist. Their eyes met. She nodded to him and started to play. His first words were still rather too soft, but after the first line, his volume increased, and those in the room began to listen with interest.

> *Over in the land of promise*
> *A garden sits quiet still*
> *And it was there where Jesus*
> *Lay down His will*
> *He prayed to His heavenly Father*
> *And said "Not my will but yours"*
> *Then He went from that garden*
> *To hell's own doors*
>
> *Bow your knee in Gethsemane*
> *To hear the word of God*
> *The cross will not be easy*
> *But He will make you strong*
> *Give your life in Gethsemane*
> *And to Jesus be true*

Then you will say to the Lord of Lords
"Not me but You"

Though the darkness abounds
And sorrow fills the air
Though the burdens may weigh you down
Jesus will be there
And in that garden fort
Where the Father watches on
The angel of the Lord
Will lift up your arm[2]

After the last note, the applause that followed was genuine but not overwhelming. In fact, his performance was a good one but had its missteps, as all performances do when the singer's mouth feels like it's full of cotton balls. After James took the requisite bow, Miss Kelly stood up from the piano and walked over to him. She leaned over to his ear and spoke loudly enough to be heard over the applause.

"From the heart," she said and then looked him in the eye. They smiled and walked off the stage in opposite directions. He sat next to John, who didn't say anything. He just looked at him, smiled, and nodded his head up and down.

At this point, the day's events were over. The award ceremony began after a ten-minute break. Everyone was milling around the auditorium when the principal stood up to the microphone and called everyone back to their seats.

"Some of you have a long trip ahead of you tonight, so we're going to get started with the awards here as soon as everyone can come back in and have a seat." Most people ignored him and kept making too much noise to hear what was happening. Only after they realized he had started a minute earlier did the room quiet down.

The list of final results was a long one. John managed to pull off first place in brass instrumentals. After receiving his blue ribbon at the front, he kissed it and held it up in the air. As he sat back down, James gave him a slight smile and nodded his head.

Lastly came the vocalist categories. The room was tense, even though the people sitting there had gone through this process each time a first-place winner was announced. For forty-five minutes, over and over for each new category, the people in the room followed the same pattern.

"In third place, from Charlotte's Trinity High School," the principal read, "Michael Jones." Everyone applauded as he walked up to receive his white ribbon.

"And in second place, from right here in Raleigh is..." The principal looked at his papers more closely to be sure, "it's James Moody." Cordial applause again as James went up front to receive his red, second-place ribbon.

"Which means that first place goes to Stephen Cameron from Greenville's Kingswood Academy!" The cheers and applause rose to a crescendo, a fitting tribute to a day that was long, weary, full of best efforts, and finally over.

People began to mill around as the principal quickly read out the congratulatory remarks and the words of thanks to all those who had "worked so hard to make the day possible."

Through all the ups and downs of the day, it was as if the air had been let out of a gigantic balloon. The people in the room were drained of all expectation, except that of a long drive home ahead of them. Friends from different schools and cities said goodbye to each other. Winners in the same category congratulated each other. And organizers and volunteer workers of the event hurried everyone else out as much as they politely could while beginning to stack chairs and tables for the inevitable clean-up.

"Oh well, James. Maybe next time," John said. "But hey! Second place is not too bad, is it?"

"Yeah, I guess so." He looked down and then back up. "See you on Monday."

"Yep, see ya then."

James looked at the red ribbon on the way home. He didn't speak much but just thought—mostly about his performance, trying to figure out how he could have made it better. He placed the award in the seat next to him and shook his head back and forth slowly.

CHAPTER 10

Losing Control

Barbara's homecoming was quite a celebration. Family and friends met her at the airport. Traveling halfway around the world and back was not something this family was used to, so it was a big event when things got back to normal.

"How are you feeling, James?" she asked as they walked out of the Raleigh-Durham Airport after the unavoidable wait at the luggage carousel.

"Fine," he said casually. "You know I won second place in the Fine Arts Festival, as a vocalist."

"Yes, Aunt Pansy told me that when I spoke to her on the phone before leaving India. I'm so proud. I wish I could have been there."

"That's okay. I guess there'll be other times."

After arriving back home, Barbara's sister handed her the keys to the house and car, a ceremonial "passing of the baton" (or a returning of the "scepter" back to the queen of the household).

"There you go, Bobbie. I guess things are back to normal now."

"I don't think things will ever be back to normal, Pansy," said

Barbara. There was a heaviness in her words that her sister immediately sensed. The two embraced, and Pansy left for her home.

"Right. What's for dinner?"

"Who are you asking, Mom?" James said.

"What are we having tonight? I'm hungry," Steve said.

• • •

About a week later, as Barbara dropped the boys off from school again, she grabbed James' wrist before he opened the door.

"James, we have an appointment with Dr. Thompson tomorrow morning. He wants to do a CAT scan on you, a check-up of sorts."

"Why? I thought I'd finished those treatments."

"Yes, you have, but he just wants to have a follow-up look and see how things are going."

The boy was uneasy about returning to the hospital, even if it was only for a couple of hours.

"Make sure you ask your teachers for the work you might miss tomorrow," she instructed. "And make sure to get work from your afternoon classes too, just in case we don't make it back to school after lunch. I've asked Peggy to take Steve with her until we can pick him up later."

"All right." He opened the door and headed to class. But his pace had slowed a little, his hands in his pockets. His hair had been growing back over the last several months, but it was still short. His

112

mother drove away, apologizing through the open window to the teacher who was directing traffic as she drove by.

By now, James was familiar with the routine of scans. He followed the technician's directions intuitively, leaning forward, taking a deep breath, not moving when he was told. After it was over, they were told to go on ahead to lunch and come back in the afternoon when the doctor would have had a chance to look at the results.

When they returned back, Dr. Thompson came into the examination room in his business-as-usual manner. He greeted them both and asked James to remove his shirt so he could prod around a bit more.

"Do you have any pain here, James?" he asked, pressing on the boy's side.

"No, not really."

"Feel anything at all, except for my cold hands?"

"No."

"Sit up and let me listen to your breathing. Sit up straight now."

The boy straightened himself as the doctor placed the stethoscope on his back.

"Now breathe in...and out...big breath in...and out..." He took the stethoscope out of his ears and handed the boy his shirt. "Okay. You can put your shirt back on right now. I'll be back in a minute, Mrs. Moody."

He walked out of the office and closed the door quietly behind him. Barbara picked up a magazine to flip through while waiting. James sat there, looking at the posters on the wall and trying to figure out what all the medical implements in the room were actually used for.

Ten minutes passed by. Then fifteen. Barbara put her magazine down. The two talked about school work. Twenty minutes. Half an hour passed. Finally, Barbara opened the door and approached one of the staff members.

"Nurse, where is Dr. Thompson?"

"Umm...I'm not sure." She looked around. The exam rooms were empty. It was after five o'clock, and most patients had already left. "He must be in his office down on the right where that door is open."

Barbara walked over to his door, and, seeing him inside with his back to her, she knocked to get his attention.

"Oh, yes," he said distractedly. "Mrs. Moody, come in."

He walked over to close the door behind her.

"Doctor, I thought you were going to give us the results of the scan."

"Mrs. Moody, you called me to do this scan if you remember."

"Yes."

"Why?"

"Because there's something wrong, and I want to find out what."

"What do you mean, 'something wrong'? How do you know that? Has the boy been complaining of pains or anything else?"

"No, but I know something isn't right."

"You can't possibly know that. Have you taken him to see another physician?"

"No, Doctor. I know that because *God* has shown me there's something wrong."

"God?" he said angrily. "God? Don't give me any of that God stuff. I don't want to hear that. I'm not interested in hearing your views on religion."

"It's not a 'view on religion,' Dr. Thompson. It's about a man named Jesus Christ."

"Oh no," he said, holding up his hand. "That is *not* what we're talking about here."

"No, it's really not. We're talking about my son, who is in there with another tumor in his body. That's what it is, isn't it, Doctor?"

The man hesitated. He looked away from her. "Yes, it is, Mrs. Moody. It's another tumor lodged in his lung—this time the size of a grapefruit. The cancer has spread again. You know, the last time it showed up in his lung, there was a tumor the size of a golf ball. The surgeon removed it successfully. This time it is much larger, and there's no way to tell if it will move again."

"Well, what are you going to do?"

"Do?" His tone became sarcastic with a tinge of anger. "You want me to go in there and tell a young man who is supposed to have the rest of his life to look forward to that things look even worse than before? Do you want me to go in there and tell him, 'Oh, don't worry, James. It will all be all right. Just keep believing in your *God*'? Because that's what I *can't* tell him, Mrs. Moody. I see people die of this stuff every day of my life. It's *not* okay. The pain and suffering of this world are all that are guaranteed to us while we live. And why some people would *want* to go on living in this world, I don't know." He looked away from her eyes at his last comment.

Barbara looked at him, looked to the wall at his many degrees and diplomas, and then looked to the ground.

"Dr. Thompson," she said slowly, her head rising up to look back at him, "all we have right now is hope. Would you take that away too? If that is all God gives us while we're alive—and I don't believe it is—then the least we can do is take hold of *that* and never let it go."

He wanted to respond but held himself back. Exasperated, he opened the door and stepped back to allow her to go out first. The two walked down to the examination room where James sat. The hallway was empty now, with the lights dimmed for the evening. He knocked on the door half-heartedly, opened it up, and let the mother enter first. Then he followed behind her.

• • •

The following week was heavy. If a cloud had descended on the family the first time they dealt with such news, this time a category five hurricane had hit them. This was the second tumor appearing in James' lung. On the first occasion, the doctors had hoped that surgical removal would contain the spread since it was small. And so, the procedure had been successful. Almost everyone had thought the worst was over at that time, that the fight had been won. Apparently not. Apparently, the quiet of the last half-year was only the calm before the storm.

His grandparents had come over for dinner. Reece and Charles were sitting in the den watching some predictable sitcom but not really engaged in the storyline. The two men were quiet and reflective.

"How's your business these days?" Reece asked, trying to make conversation as if things were the same.

"Not bad," Charles answered. "In fact, it's been pretty good at the barbershop lately. We've never been busier, at least not since before the Beatles came to America."

The two men smiled and gave a short and shallow laugh. They looked back to the television, and ten or fifteen seconds passed between them.

"Looks like James is in for another tough round of operations and treatments, Bobbie says." Reece looked to the floor while speaking, a blank stare on his face.

"Yeah. It's gonna be pretty rough, I'm afraid."

A few more seconds passed.

"You know, I pray for him every day, Charles."

"Yeah. Me too."

"Charles, you know I've given up smoking now."

"Good for you. That must have been tough."

"Well, not really. I just stopped one day. In fact, I told God that if he'd heal James, I'd just stop and never touch another. And I did."

Charles slowly nodded his head up and down with his eyes still on the television screen.

"That's a good prayer," he said thoughtfully.

"He's gonna need all the help he can get," Reece said. "But he'll come through this. I know it. He'll be all right."

"Yeah," Charles said, not sure if he could believe the sentiment or not.

After Reece and Rose left that evening, everyone else left the kitchen to go their separate ways. Steve went on to his room, and Charles had nestled into the den by now. As James placed his dishes in the sink and turned to walk out, his mother stopped him.

"James, are your things ready for tomorrow morning?"

"No, I'm not ready," he said with a little anger rising in his voice. Barbara sensed the apprehension and frustration.

"Look, I know it's not what you had planned. It's not what any of us wanted. But it's the thing we have to do right now."

"We have to do it? Don't we have a choice?" His voice was growing louder now.

"No, we don't have a choice now, Son. We can't just ignore it. It has to be dealt with."

"Why do I have to deal with it? Huh?" He was clearly angry now, and his mother served as the focal point of his frustration.

"Come over here," she coaxed. "Sit down for a minute." She walked over to him, placed her hand on his shoulder, and pulled the kitchen table chair out again. He sat down, elbows resting on the table, hands together, his forehead leaning on his thumbs which were placed in the crook of his nose. He looked into the table.

"I can't tell why it is we have to deal with things like this in life. That's not important right now. What's important is that we deal with it."

The boy said nothing but sat in silence. It was the first time he displayed this kind of exasperation during the ordeal. Even though he was sitting down, his manner was nervous, uneasy. He had endured the previous months with a silent resignation. It was not pleasant, but he knew the things had to be done if his life was to be saved.

"I'm getting tired of this."

"I know you are, James. But just hold on."

"Hold on to what?" He began to break. "I don't know what I'm supposed to do." The tears started to trickle down both sides of his face, falling onto the kitchen table below. His crying was subdued but still flowing. His mother stood up and stepped behind him, hands on his shoulders.

"What is it God wants from me?" he said between the sobs that had begun to build up.

Barbara said nothing. She had nothing to say. A couple of minutes passed. No one spoke as his tears flowed. He was the type whose tears and sobs were as silent as he could manage.

The sniffles slowed down as he wiped his face with his sleeve, and he gradually regained control of his emotions.

"I'm going outside to the swing." He got up from the table while pushing the chair back out of the way. "And maybe while I'm out there, I can just go ahead and die now."

Barbara stopped him and placed her hands on his shoulders while looking straight into his eyes.

"No, you're not!" she said, the resolve growing in her. "You're *not* going to die. You're *not* going to give up. You *will not* let this thing take your hope. We are not people who give up. We keep fighting."

He turned away, rushed out the back door slamming it behind him, and ran out to the swing that hung beneath the old tree.

Barbara, torn with her own pain, left the unwashed dishes and retreated into her own room once again. She sat in silence, flipping through the pages of her well-worn Bible, praying as she read the promises of the Psalms.

Charles walked into the kitchen shortly after. He looked at the sink full of dishes and glanced out the window at his son in the swing. He poured himself a cup of coffee, loaded it with sugar, and set it next to the coffeepot. He closed his eyes and leaned against the kitchen counter to brace himself, both hands spread out on its edge. After a few seconds, he said a prayer, took a big breath, and walked out to the front porch where he would often sit for hours just looking up into the night sky. Elm Street was quiet.

James sat in the swing, trying to get full control of his emotions again and wiping away the few remaining tears. He sat there, not really trying to move the swing, but thinking of the future. He sat, feeling the sense of control slipping away from his hands and the growing awareness of his mortality and of the unknown. What would happen? What would the future bring? How would he do all that he had wanted to do in life now? Was it possible that he really could die? It hadn't been unbearable so far—some operations, a lot of vomiting, needles, the loss of his hair. He got through it all. But it felt different this time. For the first time, he was really confronted with the possibility of not surviving. What would that be like?

Great sobs and tears started to rush in upon him again like a dam bursting its barrier. Uncontrollably, the tears spilled down his cheeks and onto the ground. He could not stop. He could not gain control of himself. He could only cry.

• • •

The operation was performed by another surgeon, Dr. Cannon. He was a balding man (a little hair on either side of the smooth, tanned top of his head). He wore circular wire-rimmed glasses, was over six feet tall, and had the personality of a ringmaster at a circus—cheerful, excited, the center of attention whenever he entered a hospital room.

During pre-operative exams, Barbara had asked him, "Well,

how much of his lung can you actually remove, Doctor?"

"All of it," he said. "And then we can start on the other one if we have to. The good Lord gave us two of lots of things, sort of as a backup if you ask me." A big grin came on his face as he patted her hand.

"We've gone through this once already," she said. "Is it going to be like last time?"

"It's a little more challenging than last time, Mrs. Moody, and you need to prepare yourself for a tough few days."

In fact, this operation was the longest and most complicated yet. He was in the operating room for six or seven hours. At the end of it, the surgeon had succeeded in removing half of the boy's left lung, the tumor itself having lodged in that lower half. Two large tubes were inserted into the side of his chest and left there to drain blood and fluid after the operation. Because he was operating on vital organs in the boy's body, he was sent straight to the Intensive Care Unit from the operating room. As he was brought in and laid on the bed, deeply unconscious and unaware of the trauma his body had just endured, his mother and father were allowed into the room sporadically to be with him.

Drips and drops of IVs, tubes, and bandages covered his body. A large tube was inserted down his throat for the respirator that lay beside his bed. His breathing was controlled not by himself but by a machine, pumping fresh oxygen in and exhaling the used air out. It sat there running relentlessly and regularly: in...out...in...out...

Hours later, as he drifted in and out of consciousness, he could hear the noise of the respirator. He was hardly aware of anything else, but he could hear that machine. He could feel something lodged in his throat, but he lay helpless to do anything about it all. He could not move. He could not turn. In fact, he could not even breathe on his own.

As the realization came to him of where he was and what he had been through, he could do nothing but lay in the bed, helpless. That evening, he closed his eyes ever so slowly and drifted off into a troubled sleep.

• • •

Days later, he was back in a regular hospital room. He had come out of the Intensive Care Unit. The respirator tube had been removed from where it had been lodged down his throat at some point when he was deemed strong enough to breathe on his own. The two tubes in his side had not been removed, though.

Dr. Cannon came into the room in his usual jovial manner, lighting up the faces of everyone who happened to be there at the time.

"So, how are we doing, James? Ready to get out of here and go play some football?"

James only smiled half-heartedly.

Reece, who was there with Barbara and her mother, spoke up: "Doctor, if that's what your operations do, then I'd like to be your next patient. I never *could* play football well, but hey..."

The doctor reached out to touch the man on the arm.

"I'll sign you up, then!"

He took a chair over to James' bedside and started to pull the sheets away.

"Now, let's have a look at these bandages. We need to make sure everything is just fine under there."

The boy followed his directions, rolling, turning, sitting still, and anything else he was told to do.

"You know these two tubes that are still here, James?"

"Yes, sir."

"Well, we don't want those things to start getting too attached to you. It doesn't look like we're going to need them anymore since they have drained away about all there is to drain. That means we're going to take them out today."

"Will it..."

"...hurt?" the surgeon finished his question. "Yes, it will, but it will only be for a few seconds. Here's what we're going to do. When we're ready, I'm going to tell you to take a deep breath and hold it in. And don't let it out until I tell you. While you're holding your breath, I'm going to pull these out. Okay?"

"All right." The boy was frightened but relieved at the same time to have things getting back to normal.

After some further preparations with the nurse standing nearby, he looked at the boy.

"Ready?"

James nodded his head.

"I'll count to three and say, 'go.' That's when you hold your breath. Okay, here we go: one-two-three-go! Take a big breath. Hold it, hold it."

James took the biggest breath he could and held it for what seemed a very long time. Dr. Cannon began to pull on the first tube. A sharp, cold sensation filled his torso, and he thought the tube must be ten feet, as it took so long to pull one out. After the doctor removed it, the nurse quickly handed him the bandages he needed to patch up the hole. He sewed up the incision he had made the week before. He pressed down to stop the bleeding and then cleaned the wound. He then followed the same procedure for the other tube.

• • •

The next week the boy was back at home in his own bed. But he would still not be in school for some time. Steve served as the messenger between school and home, taking work to James' teachers and bringing more work home for him to do as his strength allowed him.

The counsel of the team of doctors was not to follow up the surgery with radiation therapy. But further chemotherapy would be needed. Thus followed more weeks and months of the now-familiar procedure: a daily trip to Dr. Robertson's office in the morning; enjoying the company of Nurse Sandy as she stuck him and pumped him full of chemicals; a return trip home to spend the rest of the afternoon vomiting, heaving, and sleeping; and simply being exhausted from the routine of the day.

At twelve years of age, he looked only ten or eleven. At fifteen years old now, he looked not much older than he was on the day of that first visit to the doctor. The onset of puberty and adolescence had been affected. His voice had not changed. Through it all, he gained little weight and lost much of what he did gain. The sickly yellow skin color returned, his hair once again fell out, and he resorted to the use of his cap whenever he went out of the house (which was a rare thing again). Most of his time not spent in bed was spent at his drafting table, putting models together, or designing castles on paper. Or, he spent time at his piano, still trying to pick out songs he wanted to play but didn't learn from a musical score. And, of course, he would read. He fell in love with the books by Charles Dickens during warm days outside while sitting in the swing. At least in those books, he could enter into his own world.

CHAPTER 11

———

Alone in the Garden

A couple of months into his senior year of high school, Steve came in from school one day and waited until dinner to make his announcement.

"I think I'm going to join the Marine Corps." He waited for a response. It took a few seconds before anyone could.

"Well, are you *sure* about that, Steve?" his mother asked.

"Yeah. We had an aptitude test at school last month. Look—we got the results today." He handed his mother a piece of paper.

"You didn't decide this just *today*, did you? Not based on *this*?" Barbara questioned, holding up the paper.

"Well, no, of course not. But this is pretty much right on, don't you think?"

She looked at the paper and handed it to Charles, who only briefly glanced at it.

"Besides, Dad was in the Marine Corps. Somebody has to carry on the family tradition, right?"

His father smiled and looked down at his plate to get another bite of his dinner.

"I talked to the recruiters at school, but they need to speak with you two. Can we go over to the recruiting office tomorrow?"

"Well, we'll have to see *when* we can do it," Barbara replied, albeit with some reservation. "But I guess so. What do you think, Charles?"

"I think it's a fine choice, Son. I think you'll do well in the Corps. You could even make a career out of it. But you know I can't leave work to talk to them. You and your mother go over. Ask them to come over to the house one evening. I'm sure they'll do that."

The evening they did come, James had completed a new round of chemotherapy. He was so drowsy from the effects of the treatment that he slept through the day and through the night, waking only briefly to walk into the living room and see two men in uniforms talking to his parents, along with Steve.

"We think it is a great choice for a young man, Mr. Moody. I hear you were in the Corps yourself? Were you at Parris Island too?"

"No, I was living in Michigan at the time, so I was sent over to California for basic training—Camp Pendleton."

"Well, Steve won't be quite *that* far away. But I can guarantee you this: he'll be a different man when he comes back to visit you."

"Oh, I'm sure of that," his father said knowingly. A gentle smile came on his face.

• • •

As spring came, so did the warm, gentle, southern breezes of North Carolina. This Sunday was particularly gorgeous—a perfect sunny morning, nothing but deep blue skies and sunshine all around. Elm Street was quiet. The semi-hustle of downtown Raleigh's traffic that usually flares up early mornings or late afternoons was missing. Very little traffic could be heard at all. The only sounds around the neighborhood that morning were birds chirping or new, young leaves dancing in the breeze on the branches with one other.

It was Easter morning. The egg hunts had long ago been given up in the Moody household. But new Easter outfits for church had not. After breakfast, the boys and their mother dressed—James still wearing his hat. They walked up the street past three houses to their church on the corner of Polk and Elm Streets. As usual, they only made it just in time.

Sunday School was followed by a short break as everyone settled into their pews for the main service of the day. The Moodys' usual place was the second to front row on the left. Steve, of course, had long ago given up that position and sat with some other teenagers in the back. Barbara was not beyond forcing her eighteen-year-old to sit with her, though, if he ever misbehaved in the service.

The service went forward as usual, and the pastor announced the taking of the offering. While it was collected, everyone stood to sing with the choir to the accompaniment of an organ and piano.

I'm so glad I've learned to trust Thee

Precious Jesus, Savior, Friend

And I know that Thou art with me

Wilt be with me to the end

Jesus, Jesus, how I trust Him

How I've prov'd Him o'er and o'er

Jesus, Jesus, precious Jesus

O for grace to trust Him more[3]

As the music continued to play, the choir members left the platform and returned to their seats in the pews. The congregation sat down as the pastor walked up to the pulpit.

"Thank you, Sister Jones, for that music. It's a lovely way to celebrate this Easter Sunday, or as I like to call it, 'Resurrection Sunday.'" The pastor smiled broadly and looked out over his well-dressed congregation. His southern drawl was complemented by a deep, melodious tone in his voice that made him appear to be made just for the job of preacher. Too many glasses of sweet iced tea and too many plates of fried chicken legs at church socials also testified that, yes indeed, he was a preacher.

"We're so glad to have you with us today as we celebrate the most wonderful news that mankind has ever been privileged to receive—that Jesus Christ rose from the dead and holds out to each one of us the promise of eternal life as well.

"And while we rightly pay much attention to this momentous event, today I want to look at something that happened *before* our

Lord's crucifixion and *before* the resurrection. It took place in a small garden called Gethsemane, just outside the gates of Jerusalem.

"The night before Jesus was crucified, He was there with His disciples. 'Watch and pray with me,' He told them. But, of course, like some of you during my sermons, they fell asleep!"

More than a few chuckles could be heard scattered throughout the assembly.

"But what Jesus prayed on that solemn night is nothing less than ground-breaking for humanity; it is remarkable, and it is life-transforming if we could only grab hold of it and pray it from the depths of our hearts.

"You see, Jesus was about to face the most trying time of His entire life—the sufferings, the beatings, the scourging, and ultimately the crucifixion."

James, who was attentive but looking down on the floor, now looked up to the pastor. He listened closely.

"But none of that was as bad as the one thing He could not bear to think about—being separated from His Father whom He loved so dearly. You see, that's what happened when He was on the cross. God the Father could not look on sin, yet *Jesus* took upon Himself the guilt of everyone who has ever sinned against the Lord. And that's you and me. I assure you, brothers and sisters, whether you are a prince or a pauper, we're all in the same boat—sinners before Almighty God.

"Even Jesus prayed: 'Father, if it is Your will, take this cup away from Me; nevertheless...not *My* will but *Yours* be done.'" The preacher paused and looked over the faces of his sheep. "Let me ask you a question today, Friend. Who rules *your* life?"

• • •

The sun had reached its zenith now. The pastor stood on the front porch of the church building, shaking hands with his congregants. Younger children were chasing one another outside on that warm day. Some boys, shirts all untucked, were playing "king of the hill" in their Sunday best and being yelled at by their mothers *not* to play in their Sunday best. Friends stopped on the steps to ask about each other's family or to hear whatever news there was to hear.

Barbara and her sons greeted the pastor.

"Well, Steve, I hear you're leaving us soon, heading off to the Marines. Is that right?"

"Yes, sir."

"Well, I know you'll make a fine Marine. They only take the best young men, you know!"

"Thank you."

"Barbara, you have a good day, and say hello to Charles for me."

"Thank you, Pastor. I'll do that."

The three walked away. The pastor put his hand on James' shoulder as they left and winked at him.

• • •

Steve's high school graduation ceremony came far too quickly for Barbara. Students in their caps and gowns marched down the aisle of the school auditorium to a piano rendition of "Pomp and Circumstance." At the end, caps were thrown into the air, only to find sentimental mothers picking them all up, asking other nervous mothers if they had found *their* child's cap.

Summer vacation was a short one for Steve, as the Marine Corps would not wait too long for adolescence to end.

The chartered bus leaving Raleigh for Parris Island, South Carolina, departed in mid-evening, just to make sure it arrived on base after midnight. Parents were free to say goodbye to their sons as they boarded the bus near the state fairgrounds, but that would be as far as they could go.

"Well, Son. Just remember what I said to you." Charles and Steve shook hands. "Don't let them break your spirit. Follow orders, and do everything you're told. But remember who you are."

"I will, Dad."

Steve reached his hand out to his younger brother. He was, of course, much taller than the boy, over six feet tall, while James remained just over five feet.

"Thanks for bringing all that homework for me the last couple of years," James said, looking to the ground.

"Sure. What else are brothers for?" They both said goodbye uncomfortably.

James and Charles stood away a few steps. Barbara grabbed her middle son tightly and gave him one last kiss.

"Steve, I know the last few years haven't been the best or easiest for any of us. So much of my time has been taken with looking after James, and maybe I haven't spent as much time with you as I should have. But before you leave, I want you to know something. We are so proud of you. You've done so well, and we love you so much. Don't ever forget that."

"I know, Mom," he said, looking down to the ground.

She grasped him again for one final hug before her son left to become a man, to become a Marine.

The mother, father, and youngest son stood with other parents and families in the parking lot waving to the boys as they left on the warm summer night. The exhaust from the Greyhound bus hung in the air as the families, all suffering at least one loss together, slowly dispersed to their cars.

● ● ●

Towards the end of that summer, Barbara received a phone call from some friends in Virginia.

"Well, when are they supposed to be in North Carolina?...Yes, that is soon, but I guess we could have them stay with us....Yes, we can arrange a meeting here in our home. I have some friends I can invite over....Four of them?...Oh, a family with two children?... How old are they?...Okay, well, just give them my phone number, and they can call when they're ready to arrange the date...speak with you later."

A week later, a family of four arrived from England. The mother and father were complemented by an eight-year-old daughter and ten-year-old son. They arrived in August, the hottest part of the American southern summer. It was their first time in America, and nothing had prepared them for such hot, humid weather. In such circumstances, a visit to the swimming pool seemed the right thing to do.

They had prepared to have a prayer meeting in the Moody home Friday night. Barbara had invited as many of her friends as she could, and the spacious living room was used as a makeshift auditorium, James' faithful, upright piano still standing in its usual place. It would be an informal get-together of friends. They would have a chance to meet some new friends, share some music together, and encourage one another along on life's path of troubles and triumphs by sharing their own stories.

Fascinated by everything English since reading the great English novels, James was curious, excited, and eager to meet English people for the very first time. It would be his first meeting with non-Americans. More than anything, though, he was taken with their strong sense of faith and adventure. After all, here they were, traveling as missionaries throughout America, seeing new places, meeting new people, thousands of miles from their own home.

His friendship with the couple's son grew fast and thick. As they were forced into each other's company, it was an easy friendship to develop. Moreover, he was eager to find out how the English did everything, as was their son, eager to discover what life was like as an American. Though they were six years apart, their mutual interest in each other's life and experience put them both in a sympathetic and receptive position, both willing to listen and learn from the other. Besides, there was no one else they could hang out with for the time being.

The two weeks of their short stay passed all too quickly for James. Not daring to venture into friendship with others at his church or school, he was most of the time alone. These two weeks saw him make the first small steps to re-entering society—although tentatively. He was by no means ready to come out of the shell he had built for himself, but he was at least no longer an object of attention when out in public. Treatments had ceased some months before, and his physical appearance was returning to normal. Too quickly, though, the day the family was to move on arrived.

"Barbara, you've been so kind to us while we've been here," their mother Jan said in parting.

"Yes, you've been a tremendous blessing. We do appreciate it so much," Robert chimed in.

"Well, we've certainly enjoyed having you. You'll have to keep in touch with us."

"Absolutely," said the English "mum." "You know, Robert and I were talking about this last night. Why don't you and James come over to England to see us? We'll be heading back at the end of the summer. Maybe when the children are off school during their spring vacation, you could come over and speak at our church. James could sing, and the kids could see each other again."

"Maybe so," Barbara answered while a new idea began to take

shape in her thoughts. "Maybe we will. I'll have to talk with Charles about it and see what he thinks."

"Fantastic," Robert replied while closing the back end of the car. Hugs and not a few tears followed. "Come on, kids—into the old 'station wagon' as they call it here. Cheerio, folks!"

"Goodbye," Barbara called out.

James was quiet. "See you, Matthew. Enjoy the rest of your trip."

"See you. Maybe next time in England!"

• • •

At the end of that summer, James started his junior year in high school. Things went relatively smoothly. He no longer took part in PE classes due to his ongoing weaknesses, but in almost every other class, he was fully engaged. He even had enough spare energy for a little extra-curricular activity, including writing for the school newspaper. His first article, "Are Brown Bananas Better than Yellow Bananas?" didn't seem to have the grand effect he had hoped. But there it was anyway.

What really made the year worthwhile, though, was English class. It was his first year with the high school English teacher, Mrs. Savage.

A truly genteel, southern belle of a lady, the middle-aged teacher fed his love for reading and writing like no one else in the school had. Her constant encouragement, her strict enforcement of the discipline of reading, and her explanations of the mechanics and the feeling of literature found a home in the boy's heart and personality. Though he didn't grasp everything she taught or said, he imbibed the love of reading and learning that was an apparent part of her own life. Books, learning, and communication were becoming to him, not just a discipline that had to be learned but a pleasure that got to be enjoyed. And to cap off this junior year (which focused on the literature of England), his father and mother had decided that she and James *would* travel to England in the spring after all.

The only drawback to the trip was he would have to leave the baby grand piano that his father recently purchased for him. It was exquisite—black and shiny with a sound to equal anything in Carnegie Hall (at least to *him*, though he'd never been to Carnegie Hall). It was beyond his dreams that he would ever be able to own and play such a lofty instrument. Compared with his old four-hundred-dollar saloon special, the second-hand black beauty was like a Rolls Royce sitting next to a scooter. It was beyond imagining, but here it was in the living room of their house.

In the end, though, not even the piano could hold him back from the remarkable adventure now before him—traveling to the mythical land of Great Britain.

CHAPTER 12

——◆——

First Flight

They arrived at Gatwick Airport just south of London early in the morning.

"Barbara! James! Over here!"

The whole family was there to greet the travelers at the International Arrivals Hall. They waved frantically, the children running up to meet them.

"Well, how was your first trans-Atlantic flight, James?" Robert asked.

"Not bad," the boy answered. "I'm pretty tired, though," he replied, trying to adjust himself to his very first flight and the traveler's baptism, otherwise known as "jet lag."

"I'm afraid there's a terrible accident on the M-25, the main motorway that gets us around London," Jan explained. "We're going to have to take the scenic route along the back roads. It might take a little longer, but at least you'll see more of the countryside!"

"Whatever you say," Barbara agreed, herself starting to feel the jet lag. "We're in your hands."

They reached the car, and the American travelers looked in surprise.

"Well, here we are. This is our Austin Maxi. I'm afraid it's a little small—nowhere near the size of the Oldsmobile 'station wagon' we used in America. But I'm sure the six of us can fit in there with no problem."

To American eyes, the brown, aging, English car would be considered a sub-compact. It was pretty much standard for European roads. But even the close quarters of a five-hour drive through the countryside could not dampen James' excitement about actually being in England. To him, everything was new, amazing, and beautiful—an adventure to be lived, rather than a limitation. He drank in the images of the countryside, sitting in the backseat squeezed tightly next to his friends.

The rolling hills covered in fresh, green grass seemed endless. The sheep grazing and lambing were plentiful. And the sun shining down on an array of wild and planted flowers was unusually abundant for those two weeks. Not a drop of rain came in sight for the whole time of their trip.

They would be staying in South Wales, so the drive from Gatwick Airport was indeed a long one. James fought the urge to sleep so he could see every part of it. Arriving in the small town of Llanelli, Robert pulled the car onto the sidewalk so they could all unload the luggage.

The house was a large, semi-detached building, probably built in the Edwardian age. It was a stucco building with a moderately-sized back garden, large enough for rabbit hutches and space to kick a soccer ball.

The large picture window in the kitchen, which faced the backyard, allowed plenty of sunshine to enter at sunset, providing the clouds could be kept at bay (not a typical thing for Wales).

The first night was an early one, given everyone's exhaustion from air travel and cross-country car journeys. James was given Matthew's bedroom, fully decked out with the boy's Manchester United soccer poster and paraphernalia. Matthew and his sister were to sleep in their parents' room, while Barbara was given Susan's room.

James lay in bed that night, tired to the bone but still not able to get to the sleep he so needed. His thoughts turned to the fact that he was now lying in a house in another country—a nation he had longed to see for so many years.

"I can't believe I'm here," he said to himself. "I never thought..."

Eventually, he fell asleep and slept one of the deepest and most refreshing nights of sleep he had in years past.

• • •

"Well, here's the plan," Robert explained as they all sat at breakfast the next day. "We'll stay here for the next four days and take you up to one of Wales' famous valleys that is just gorgeous this time of year. This Sunday, Barbara, you will be speaking at our local church, and James can sing. How does that sound?"

"That's fine," Barbara replied.

"In the meantime, we can do some things around town as well. They have a great swimming pool just down the road, and the coast is not too far away, either. There are some great beaches, but I'm sure you'll not be wanting to get into the water this time of year."

"I'm sure I'd not want to get in the water there, *any* time of year," Matthew said. "It's not really as warm as it is in America, is it?"

Ignoring his son's comments, Robert carried on, "Then what do you think about going to Scotland?"

"Scotland?" James asked with excitement.

"Yes," Robert said casually. "Barbara, didn't you tell me you have some relatives up in Peterhead, just north of Aberdeen?"

"Yes, we do. I haven't seen them in years, you know. The last time was when they lived in America, down in Texas."

"Well, we know a pastor in that town," said Jan.

"Yes, he might be willing to let us come speak at their church. I'll get in touch with him," Robert said. "And, why don't you get in touch with your relatives up there? Maybe they have somewhere we could stay."

"Well, they do have a block of apartments right in the town on Love Lane. Maybe they'll have one empty. I'll call them up and see what they say."

So, the itinerary was set. The boys went out into the backyard to kick a soccer ball around. Susan stuck to Barbara like cling film, wanting to show her everything in her room and explain all the different posters, dolls, and toys she had.

After lunch, the family traveled to the shops nearby to pick up some groceries and start making preparations for the long trip from Wales to Scotland. They would be traveling almost the whole length of the island of Great Britain.

• • •

After dinner that night, there seemed to be an unusual sense of peace, calm, and serenity hovering around the house. It was more than just the feeling of a family that was content with one another and at peace with one another. It was a special tranquillity that everyone intuitively felt.

After the washing up was done, everyone just lingered around the kitchen table talking.

"Okay, guys, why don't we pray?" Robert said. "We can ask God to be with us on the trip we have ahead and look after us."

"Yes," Jan said. "We need to pray about that, but there's something more we need to do, isn't there? I felt it all afternoon, but I can't quite put my finger on it. Why don't we just pray right here, in the kitchen, right now?"

Everyone agreed. The six of them stood in the center of the rather large kitchen. The night was warm, so the windows were open. The sun was just starting to set. There was an amber light filtering into the room. Each person closed his eyes and grew quiet for the first minute—even the children. That sense of abundant tranquillity seemed to increase as they stood there. It was as if a warm, quilted blanket had slowly descended upon each one of them, wrapping them in a sense of stillness, peace, and comfort.

Robert began to pray out loud. Soon the others joined in, simply speaking what was in their hearts, without premeditation, without forethought. They simply offered what was in their souls to God. James stood among them, listening, waiting, praying.

Soon, he came to sense something he had never felt before. He stood with his eyes closed, focusing all thoughts and prayers on Jesus. He began to sense what seemed like an electrical current on his head. He knew that what was happening was not of his own doing or that of anyone else in the room. The sensation grew stronger as the focus of his thoughts grew clearer.

In his mind's eye, he began to see an image. It was not something he wanted. It came unbidden to him. It was a vision of something he knew was at the root of his life, but he had not been willing to surrender. It was not what he would have chosen for himself, but he knew—without a doubt—it was the one thing in his life that God desired of him—the absolute surrender of his life to the will of God.

In his mind's eye, he saw himself standing on a platform somewhere in front of a crowd of people. He was dressed in a black suit holding a microphone...and a Bible. He stood there, preaching to the group of people who were there to hear about Jesus Christ.

James knew what it meant. He knew the step he had to take.

"God, if that is what *you* want, then that is what I want. Whether I live or whether I die, God, let my life be in *your* hands."

At the instant of that prayer, it was as if a bolt of lightning had struck him. Though it could not be seen with human eyes, the effect was the same. He had been impacted by a power and a force like he had never before experienced. He realized it was God's Holy Spirit and that something tremendous had happened to him.

He had been touched forever. He had been changed forever. He was marked forever. He was not the same person he was moments before. In fact, he was not the same sick person he had been years before.

"What happened, James?" others asked moments later.

It was fifteen or twenty minutes before he could regain his composure. He struggled to put into words what he had experienced.

"What was that? I heard something, but I don't know what," Jan added.

"I...I saw myself when I was praying...and then...then I felt..." He put his head in his hands, rubbing his eyes, and shaking himself. Having an intuitive sense of what had just happened but not being able to explain how, he said simply, "I've just been healed! God just healed me! I know it!"

"What? Are you sure?"

"Yes, I felt this...I felt...I can't really explain it now...but I know it was God who healed me. I just *know* it!"

The others gathered around. They said prayers of thanks. They sang.

In fact, their celebration was so boisterous that the neighbors came running over to the house, knocking on the door frantically.

"What's happening over here? We heard some singing coming out of your windows that was out of this world. It sounded like angels! What's going on, Robert?"

The group looked at the stunned neighbors and started to laugh and celebrate even more. "Come on in," Jan said. "We'll tell you about it over a cup of tea."

• • •

The end of the two-week, life-changing adventure into foreign lands and heavenly places ended sooner than James had hoped—from the valleys of Wales to the Highlands of Scotland (and all of England in between). It was a consolation to know that his friends would return once again to America in the summertime and that he would have the chance to be back in England—at least through them. The parting was hard, though.

On the last night following dinner, they all took a walk behind the house into the country lanes and paths across some of the greenest hills around. The rain had held off yet another day, and the sun was still just above the horizon but on its final descent. The daffodils were in full bloom, the yellow flowers complementing so vividly the deep green of the grassy fields. The calm breeze was just enough to make the blooms wobble ever so slightly as they stood firm, their roots having survived the harsh trials of winter.

The ladies were walking apart, twenty feet or so behind James and Robert. Matthew and Susan had run on ahead, eager to get to one of the secret places in the woods that "nobody else had ever been to." It was their own private, hidden piece of the world veiled from all others. Robert took the opportunity to encourage James.

"James, you know that your life has been given to you twice now. You're no longer free to live as you want or do what you want to do. You have a purpose and a calling. And that's a heavy responsibility as well as an awesome privilege." The boy looked over at him, hands in his pockets but not saying a word. "God has given you the task of taking His healing love to those in this world who are hurting."

They both stopped walking. Some stray sheep were wandering in the field, away from the rest of the flock. They watched as the younger ones dared to amble over a little closer to their location; then, they ran away once they caught full sight of the people.

"But I will tell you this, James. Once you give your life to God in this way, you'll never find anything more fulfilling in all your life."

James, still overwhelmed with all that had taken place for the last two weeks, allowed a smile to come on his face, if only slightly. It was the first time in many years he'd been able to do that authentically because it was the first time in years he actually felt such a sense of completeness, of wholeness, of healing. It was the first time, in many years, that he could feel *anything* that wonderful.

They caught up to the children who were already playing at their "secret" fort just at the edge of the woods. The games and fun began in earnest now, as the "baddies" lined up against the "goodies" and the scramble for control of the kingdom began.

• • •

After returning to America, James saw Dr. Robertson only a few more times for regular check-ups. After the final yearly check-up, he was released from the doctor's care.

"Now, I don't want to see you back here again, James," said this man with a big smile on his face. It was one of the few times he could share that expression with his patients.

"Nothing personal, Doctor, but I don't want to see *you* again either!"

• • •

The years ahead were not a walk in the park, but he was alive. He was alive to pursue a new course in life and to aim at fulfilling the purposes for which God had spared him in this world.

His music began to develop as he started to write his own songs and find other young musicians with whom to create music. Each opportunity that came along to share the remarkable acts of God in His life—whether inside the church or outside of it—he took. Studying was a pleasure. Each learning situation was like a new lease of life. Each *day* was like a new lease on life because he realized that, in fact, it truly was.

High school graduation came and went. Enrolment at university came. And though it was an entirely new world, the sense of fulfillment he enjoyed as he rode his bike to and from the campus each day could not be contained. This was life, a life that was *lived* every day.

Epilogue

One afternoon, sitting in a piano practice room while at college, James was fiddling with a tune he wanted to develop. It just would not stop playing in his head. He sat down at the piano and began to pick around, playing various riffs and picking out chord arrangements to match.

A head appeared at the door of the small practice room. It was a friend from college. "You coming to dinner now, James? I hear the cafeteria has lasagne tonight."

"Not yet," he replied. "I want to work on something for a few more minutes. Maybe I'll see you over there later."

"Better hurry up, or there won't be anything *left* if I have something to do with it."

The head disappeared as fast as it had materialized. James closed the door to shut out the noise of the hustle and bustle of the hallway. He sat back down at the piano and continued to pick around on the keys, hoping to get the sound he heard out of his mind onto the piano keyboard.

As he sat, re-playing bits and pieces of the song, trying to fit them all together, he once again began to feel that wonderful tranquillity come over him—the same sensation he felt on that incredible night in Wales. A supernatural warmth spread over him. His mind seemed to kick into high gear. His senses had been raised to a new level. His perceptions had entered into a turbo-boosted zone, and from deep within himself, he sensed a power and presence that was not of his own making.

In an instant, lyrics of a song flooded his mind. The sound of the music filled his spirit. The elements of it all came together as if the pieces of a giant jigsaw puzzle descended from the sky and were gently placed simultaneously together to make one beautiful whole—a picture that shone in his mind's eye. At the same time, it was as if he were eating a feast of manna as his soul fed from the table of heaven.

He wrote and played furiously. The springs of joy overtook even him. The tears came pouring out as the healing peace flooded in. Something more than writing a song was taking place. The truth and reality of the song and its tune acted like a healing balm on his own soul, his own mind and heart. His body had been healed. Now, the soul that had been hurt, damaged, and wounded, was being restored, healed, and given new life.

Twenty minutes later, he sat there astonished; tears brushed away from his face. The light of heaven seemed to fill his soul, his heart, his mind. It seemed the very room in which he sat at this piano in an obscure part of a college campus had become the center of the universe that night as God's presence came in.

• • •

Many years later, a man dressed in a black suit stood behind a pulpit in a church one Sunday. His voice was rather high and a little odd. He didn't have the kind of face that would make anyone take a second look. But his blue eyes were clear and filled with joy and hope. Tiny tattooed dots were imprinted into various parts of his neck—not too obvious to the casual observer, but still there. Scars of various sizes and lengths were engraved at assorted locations of his head and torso, scars that would remain there through the ages.

And in his voice could be heard the words and the heart of understanding and compassion. In his manner, there was a delivery of sincerity, of truth, and of deeply felt emotion. He knew what nighttime was like for the soul, a soul set adrift without hope. He also knew the song that could get a hurting soul through the nighttime.

He spoke urgently to the assembled crowd of listeners.

"...it doesn't *matter* what challenges you face, what pains you've endured. You need to know there is an answer. There is hope...there is healing.

"I want to tell you about a man from a place called Nazareth. His name is Jesus Christ. He is the Lord God Almighty. And He is a healer, *like no other...*"

ENDNOTES

1. "In the Sweet By and By," by S. Fillmore Bennett (1868) Public Domain

2. "Gethsemane," by James Moody (copyright 1987)

3. "Tis so Sweet to Trust in Jesus," by Louisa M.R. Stead (1882) Public Domain

ABOUT THE AUTHOR

James Moody began his adolescence in a battle for life. Through those challenges, he learned the secret of God's plan for the seeking heart. In the midst of these storms, he began to write songs that inspire the heart and encourage the hopeless. The desire to share this message with others led him to tour schools and churches of Great Britain, singing his own songs to thousands of young people across that nation. From the poorest and most deprived areas of the nation to some of the wealthiest, he shared the message with many who had lost all hope. After several years back in America, he eventually returned to England to serve as a teacher at two of England's top prep schools, instructing the next generation of leaders in the knowledge of the Scriptures. He continues to proclaim the healing presence of Jesus to those with ears to hear and hearts that are open to the love of God.

Visit online:

JamesMoody.info

Write:

James Moody
P.O. Box 735
New Bern, N.C. 28563
U.S.A.

CPSIA information can be obtained
at www.ICGtesting.com
Printed in the USA
BVHW090855080222
628399BV00018B/767